OXFORD

GCSE Maths
For Edexcel
FOUNDATION

SUPPORT WORKBOOK

OXFORD
UNIVERSITY PRESS

Ray Allan
Martin Williams

OXFORD
UNIVERSITY PRESS

Great Clarendon Street. Oxford OX2 6DP

Oxford University Press is a department of the University of Oxford.

It furthers the University's objective of excellence in research, scholarship, and education by publishing worldwide in

Oxford New York

Auckland   Cape Town   Dar es Salaam   Hong Kong   Karachi
Kuala Lumpur   Madrid   Melbourne   Mexico City   Nairobi
New Delhi   Shanghai   Taipei   Toronto

With offices in

Argentina   Austria   Brazil   Chile   Czech Republic   France   Greece
Guatemala   Hungary   Italy   Japan   Poland   Portugal   Singapore
South Korea   Switzerland   Thailand   Turkey   Ukraine   Vietnam

British Library Cataloguing in Publication Data

Data available

ISBN: 978-0-19-912886-0

10 9 8 7 6 5 4 3

Printed in Great Britain by Ashford Colour Press Ltd, Gosport

The image on the cover is reproduced courtesy of photodisc

Paper used in the production of this book is a natural, recyclable product made from wood grown in sustainable forests. The manufacturing process conforms to the environmental regulations to the country of origin.

About this book

Oxford GCSE Maths for Edexcel is a complete course designed to match the Edexcel GCSE specifications in Mathematics, for both linear and modular routes. It is based on targeted outcomes, with books at four distinct ability levels and accompanying software.

This workbook supports and consolidates the key ideas contained within the Foundation student book, which is targeted at grades E-G. The activities in this workbook consolidate learning at grades F and G, to prepare the ground for tackling the fuller topics within the textbook. It is organised into single-page exercises that are designed to be written on, and relate directly to the chapters in the student book. The order of topics reflects the linear book, but can be used equally well with the modular book by re-ordering the sections.

The exercises are self-contained so they can be used for homework, or used outside of the *Oxford GCSE Maths for Edexcel* scheme. Full answers are available on the OUP website at
www.oxfordsecondary.co.uk/maths/FBanswers

The grids below summarise the order of chapters.

Linear route	
N1	Properties of number
G1	Measures, length and area
A1	Expressions
N2	Integer calculations
G2	Angles and 2-D shapes
N3	Fractions and percentages
D1	Probability
A2	Functions and graphs
D2	Collecting data
G3	2-D and 3-D shapes
A3	Sequences
N4	Fractions and decimals
G4	Transformations
A4	Formulae and real-life graphs
N5	Powers, roots and primes
D3	Displaying data
A5	Equations
G5	Further transformations
N6	Ratio and proportion
A6	Further equations
G6	Measuring and constructing
N7	Decimal calculations
D4	Averages and range
D5	Further probability
G7	Further geometry

Modular route	
N1	Properties of number
D1	Probability
D2	Collecting data
N2	Integer calculations
D3	Displaying data
D4	Averages and range
N3	Fractions and percentages
D5	Further probability
G1	Measures, length and area
A1	Expressions
N4	Fractions and decimals
A2	Functions and graphs
G2	Angles and 2-D shapes
N5	Powers, roots and primes
A3	Sequences
G3	2-D and 3-D shapes
A4	Formulae and real-life graphs
N6	Ratio and proportion
G4	Transformations
A5	Equations
N7	Decimal calculations
G5	Further transformations
A6	Further equations
G6	Measuring and constructing
G7	Further geometry

Contents

N1a   Place value

1 a   2 5 7   What figure is shown in the hundreds column?   *2*

b   6 0 7   What figure is shown in the units column?   ....

c   4 1 9   What figure is shown in the tens column?   ....

d   3 5 4 8   What figure is shown in the thousands column?   ....

e   6 0 8 1   What figure is shown in the hundreds column?   ....

f   7 4 8 · 6   What figure is shown in the tens column?   ....

2 What score is shown on each target?

a 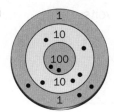   **b** 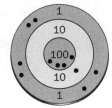   **c**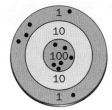

.... points   .... points   .... points

3 Answer these problems.

a 25 × 10 = ...	**b** 420 ÷ 10 = ...	**c** 19 × 10 = ...
d 640 ÷ 10 = ...	**e** 8.6 × 10 = ...	**f** 97 ÷ 10 = ...
g 5.4 × 100 = ...	**h** 357 ÷ 100 = ...	**i** 0.8 × 10 = ...

4 Write your answers from question 3 in order. Start with the smallest.

a ....   **b** ....   **c** ....   **d** ....   **e** ....

f ....   **g** ....   **h** ....   **i** ....

1 What numbers are missing from these scales?

a

| 0 | 5 | ...... | 15 | 20 | ...... | ...... | 35 |

b

| 200 | ...... | ...... | 500 | 600 | ...... | 800 |

2 What readings do these scales show?

a

16 ↑ 17

.... C°

b

220 ↑ 230

.... volts

c

3 ↑ 4

.... cm

d

0 ↑ 1

.... kg

3 Arrow 'A' points at 1.3

0   1   2   3   4   5   6

↑
A

a Draw arrows to point at:
   B = 3.7   C = 4.8   D = 5.2   E = 0.6   F = 6.5

b Label each arrow.

4 Arrow 'P' points at 88

50   60   70   80   90   100   110   120

↑
P

a Draw arrows to point at:
   Q = 73   **R** = 59   **S** = 101   **T** = 109   **U** = 48

b Label each arrow.

1 Arrow 'A' points at −3°C on this temperature scale.

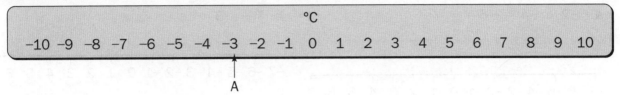

°C

−10 −9 −8 −7 −6 −5 −4 −3 −2 −1 0 1 2 3 4 5 6 7 8 9 10

A

a Draw and label arrows to show these temperatures:

B = 3°C   C = −5°C   D = 2°C   E = −2°C   F = −7°C   G = 0°C

b What is the lowest temperature? .... °C

c What is the highest temperature? .... °C

d How many degrees difference are there between
the highest and lowest temperature? .... °C

2 A thermometer is checked every 5 hours. The reading at 5am shows −7°C.

a Shade in each thermometer to show the temperature.

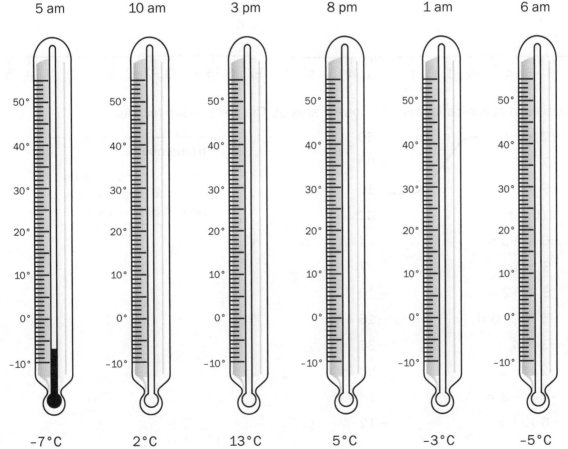

5 am	10 am	3 pm	8 pm	1 am	6 am
−7°C	2°C	13°C	5°C	−3°C	−5°C

b Does the temperature rise or fall between 5 am and 10 am? ....

c Does the temperature rise or fall between 8 pm and 6 am? ....

d How many degrees difference are there between 10 am and 3 pm? ....

e How many degrees difference are there between 5 am and 10 am? ....

f How many degrees difference are there between 8 pm and 6 am? ....

1 Use the number lines to answer these problems.

a $-2 + -4 = -6$

b $7 + -3 =$ ....

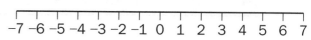

c $-5 - -4 =$ ....

d $2 - -5 =$ ....

e $6 + -11 =$ ....

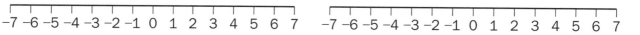

f $-4 + -3 =$ ....

g $-7 - -11 =$ ....

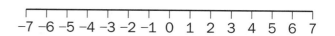

h $0 - -5 =$ ....

2 Match each multiplication with the correct answer. The first is done for you.

a $-2 \times -5 =$	-50	
b $-7 \times 2 =$	-20	
c $5 \times -4 =$	10	
d $-10 \times 5 =$	32	
e $-6 \times -3 =$	-14	
f $8 \times 4 =$	27	
g $8 \times -2 =$	-10	
h $-5 \times -10 =$	-16	
i $-3 \times 4 =$	-36	
j $2 \times -5 =$	50	
k $-9 \times -3 =$	18	
l $-6 \times 6 =$	-12	

> **Remember:**
>
> minus × minus = plus
> minus × plus = minus
> plus × plus = plus

1 Round each number to the nearest **10**, then the nearest **100**. The first is done for you.

Number		Rounded to the nearest 10	Rounded to the nearest 100
a	178	→ 180	→ 200
b	136		
c	355		
d	718		
e	962		
f	3523		
g	2454		
h	6071		
i	1798		

2 Here are average attendances over one year in top European football leagues.
Round each average to the nearest 1000.

England   -   Premiership   35 600   ≈ ....

Germany -   Bundesliga   42 565   ≈ ....

Spain   -   La Liga   29 124   ≈ ....

Italy   -   Serie A   25 504   ≈ ....

France   -   Ligue 1   24 050   ≈ ....

3 a ┌────────────────────────────────────┐
    │ I am 14 years, 2 months and 8 days old! │
    └────────────────────────────────────┘
         Round off this statement to the nearest **year**. ....

  b ┌─────────────────┐
    │ I am 176 cm tall. │
    └─────────────────┘
         Round off this statement to the nearest **10 cm**. ....

  c ┌──────────────────────────────┐
    │ She collected £31.48 for charity. │
    └──────────────────────────────┘
         Round off this statement to the nearest **pound**. ....

  d ┌───────────────────────────────────────┐
    │ I threw the shot 9 metres and 61 centimetres. │
    └───────────────────────────────────────┘
         Round off this statement to the nearest **metre**. ....

  e ┌──────────────────────────┐
    │ I weigh 53 and a half kilos. │
    └──────────────────────────┘
         Round off this statement to the nearest **kilogram**. ....

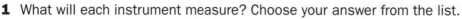

1 What will each instrument measure? Choose your answer from the list.

a  **b**  **c** 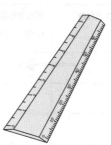 **d**

length
mass
time
capacity

....

2 Group the units of measure in the correct columns. Use the words from the list.

Capacity	Mass	Length
....	....	....
....	....	....
....	....	....
	....	....

metre
milligram
tonne
litre
millimetre
millilitre
kilometre
centilitre
kilogram
centimetre
gram

3 Choose the correct unit from each list to complete the sentence.

a When I was born I weighed 3.2 .... (*grams – metres – kilograms*)

b Tara ran 100 metres in 16.7 .... (*minutes – seconds – hours*)

c My pencil is about 15 .... long. (*centimetres – milligrams – litres*)

d A bull elephant can weigh 8 .... (*kilograms – tonnes – litres*)

e I threw a cricket ball 34 .... (*millimetres – kilograms – metres*)

4 Choose sensible units to complete this piece of text.

On a jumbo jet flight from London to New York, a distance of 5585 ....,

the journey takes 6 .... The plane will use 76 500 .... of

fuel, flying at a speed of 927 .... per hour.

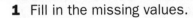
1 Fill in the missing values.

a .... mm = 1 cm   b .... g = 1 kg   c .... ml = 1 cl

.... cm = 1 m   .... kg = 1 t   .... cl = 1 l

.... m = 1 km

2 a What is the total weight of these boxes in kilograms ?

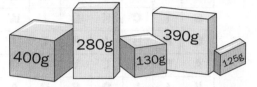

= ....

b What is the total amount of cola in litres?

= ....

c What is the total length of rope in kilometres?

= ....

d What is the total weight in tonnes?

= ....

3 a

Ten identical boxes weigh 1.2 kg.
How much does each box weigh?

= ....

b

2 metres of ribbon is cut into 5 equal pieces.
How many centimetres long is each piece?   = ...

c

One tonne of cement is loaded into 50 kg bags.
How many bags will be filled?   = ...

1 Find as many of these metric and imperial units as you can in 5 minutes. The words are written across and down. The first is done for you.

CENTIMETRE
FOOT
GALLON
GRAM
INCH
KILOGRAM
KILOMETRE
LITRE
~~METRE~~
MILE
MILLILITRE
OUNCE
PINT
POUND
YARD

G	M	I	L	L	I	L	I	T	R	E
C	E	N	T	I	M	E	T	R	E	X
S	T	C	K	B	I	W	K	Q	N	V
C	R	H	I	K	L	I	T	R	E	P
A	E	M	L	Y	E	G	J	F	T	I
K	I	L	O	G	R	A	M	P	G	N
U	R	F	M	R	A	L	F	O	O	T
C	T	Z	E	A	N	L	B	U	U	R
V	R	E	T	M	Y	O	S	N	N	E
K	Y	A	R	D	D	N	F	D	C	W
C	O	J	E	F	S	B	R	H	E	D

Length	Mass	Capacity
2.5 cm ≈ 1 inch	1 kg ≈ 2.2 pounds	600 ml ≈ 1 pint
30 cm ≈ 1 foot (12 inches)	30g ≈ 1 ounce	1 litre ≈ 1.75 pints
1 m ≈ 1 yard (3 feet)		4.5 litres ≈ 1 gallon
8 km ≈ 5 miles		

2 Rewrite each sentence converting imperial units into metric.

a Carla drove **20 miles** and used **2 gallons** of petrol.

Carla drove .... *and used* .... *of petrol*

b Dino bought **2 yards** of chain, **5 pints** of oil and **10 ounces** of wax.

Dino bought .... *of chain,* .... *of oil and* .... *of wax.*

c Joe was **6 feet** tall and weighed **176 pounds**.

Joe was .... *tall and weighed* ....

3 Rewrite each sentence converting metric units into imperial.

a Jack ran **16 kilometres** with a rucksack that weighed **10 kilograms**.

Jack ran .... *with a rucksack that weighed* ....

b Rita buys **4 kilograms** of apples, **75 grams** of yeast and **4 litres** of milk.

Rita buys .... *of apples,* .... *of yeast and* .... *of milk.*

1 Fill in the missing values on these scales.

a

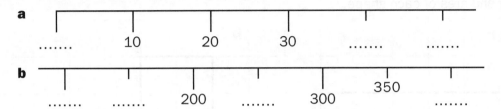

....   10   20   30   ....

b

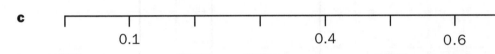

....   200   300   350   ....

c

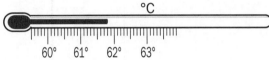

....   0.1   ....   0.4   ....   0.6

2 a What is the temperature? ....

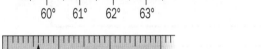

°C

60°   61°   62°   63°

b What is the weight? ....

0   1   3
Grams

c What is the weight? ....

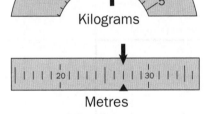

2   3   4   5
Kilograms

d What is the length? ....

20   30
Metres

500

400

300

200

Millilitres

e What is the volume? ....

3 The dials show the temperatures of the four engines of a jet airliner.

Engine 1   Engine 2   Engine 3   Engine 4

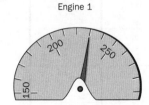 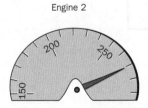 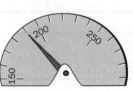 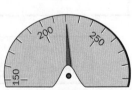

Engine Temperatures °C

a What is the temperature of engine number 1? ....

b Which engine is the hottest? ....

c Which engine is the coolest? ....

d What is the temperature of engine number 4? ....

e What is the difference in temperature between the hottest and coldest engine? ....

G1e Perimeter and area 1

These shapes are drawn on a 1 centimetre grid.
Give the perimeter and area of each shape.

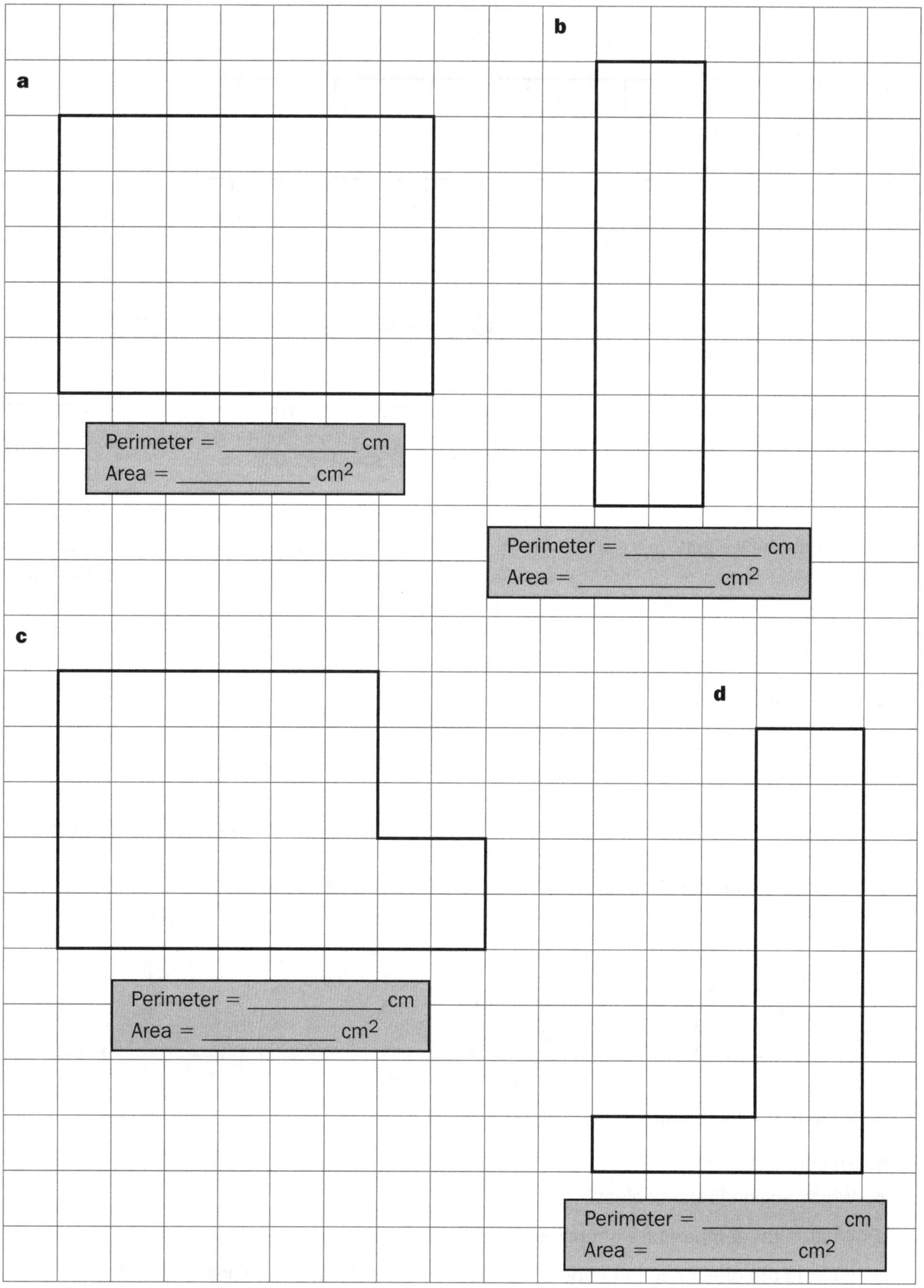
a
Perimeter = ____________ cm
Area = ____________ cm^2
b
Perimeter = ____________ cm
Area = ____________ cm^2
c
Perimeter = ____________ cm
Area = ____________ cm^2
d
Perimeter = ____________ cm
Area = ____________ cm^2

1 These shapes are drawn on a centimetre grid. What is the area and perimeter of each shape?

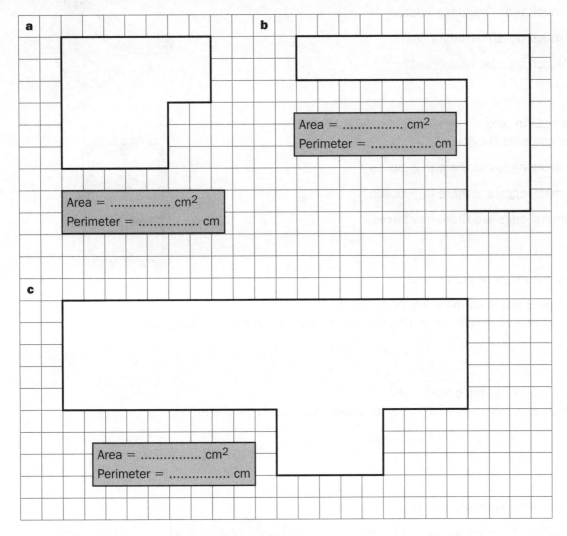

a

Area = ... cm^2
Perimeter = ... cm

b

Area = ... cm^2
Perimeter = ... cm

c

Area = ... cm^2
Perimeter = ... cm

2 Calculate the area and perimeter of each shape.

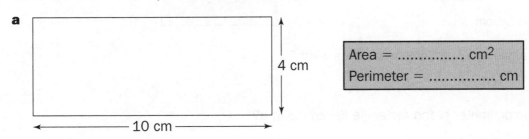

a

4 cm

10 cm

Area = ... cm^2
Perimeter = ... cm

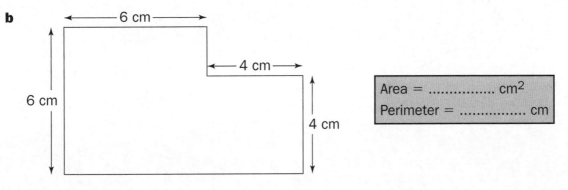

b

6 cm

4 cm

6 cm

4 cm

Area = ... cm^2
Perimeter = ... cm

1 Bananas cost 35 pence each.

   a How much will 3 bananas cost? ....

   b How much do 10 bananas cost? ....

   c How much do n bananas cost? ....

2 Eggs are sold in boxes.
Each box contains 6 eggs.

   a How many eggs are there in 3 boxes? ....

   b How many eggs are there in 5 boxes? ....

   c How many eggs are there in x boxes? ....

3 Chris has n number of polo shirts.

   a Sally has **3 times** as many shirts as Chris.
Write an expression in terms of n for the number of shirts that Sally has.

   ....

   b Hiro has 5 more shirts than Sally.
Write an expression in terms of n for the number of Hiro's shirts.

   ....

4 The width of this rectangle is x cm.

   a Its length is 5 cm longer than its width
How long is the rectangle?

   .... cm

   x cm

   b If the rectangle is 12 cm long, what is its width?

   ....cm

   c What is the perimeter of the rectangle described in **b**?

   ....cm

1 Simplify each expression by adding or subtracting.
The first one is done for you.

   a 5 dogs + 3 dogs = 8 dogs

   b 10 pens + 7 pens = ...

   c 8 bananas − 3 bananas = ...

   d 6 dice + 14 dice = ...

   e 20 books − 13 books = ...

2 Collect these terms to simplify the expressions.
The first one is done for you.

   a $x + x + x = 3x$

   b $m + m + m + m + m + m =$ ....

   c $q + q + q + q + q + q + q + q + q =$ ....

   d $t + t + t + t =$ ....

   e $h + h + h + h + h + h + h + h =$ ....

3 Collect the terms to simplify the expressions.
The first one is done for you.

   a $4n + 7n = 11n$ **b** $2v + 5v =$ ....

   c $6y + 7y + y =$ ....   **d** $2x + 9x + 3x =$ ....

   Be careful to look for the subtractions in these.

   e $15t − 10t =$ ....   **f** $12r + 6r − 2r =$ ....

   g $6z − 4z + 3z =$ ....   **h** $20p − 5p − 6p =$ ....

4 Write these expressions in their simplest form.
The first three are done for you.

   a $6 \times x = 6x$ **b** $m \div 4 = \frac{m}{4}$ **c** $b \times g = bg$

   d $g \div 7 =$ ....   **e** $20 \times j =$ ....   **f** $h \times 9 =$ ....

   g $m \times n =$ ....   **h** $q \times k =$ ....   **i** $t \div v =$

1 If $x = 5$, calculate the value of these expressions.
The first two are done for you.

    a $x + x + x = 5 + 5 + 5 = 15$

    b $4x = 4 \times 5 = 20$

    c $x + 3 = $ ....

    d $5x = $ ....

    e $3x - 2 = $ ....

    f $6x + 7 = $ ....

    g $20x = $ ....

    h $20x - 10 = $ ....

2 Calculate the value of these expressions if $y = 3$ and $w = 6$.

    a $5y = $ ....

    b $10w = $ ....

    c $5y + 5 = $ ....

    d $4w + 3 = $ ....

    e $w + y = $ ....

    f $w - y = $ ....

    g $5w + y + 2 = $ ....

    h $2w + 2y = $ ....

    i $w - 2y = $ ....

3 Calculate the perimeters of these rectangles for $x = 4$ (do not measure).

    a $3x$ cm
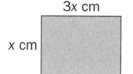
    x cm

    b $2x + 1$ cm
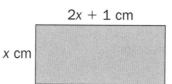
    x cm

    Perimeter = ... cm

    Perimeter = ... cm

    c $3x - 2$ cm
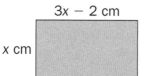
    x cm

    d $4x - 3$ cm
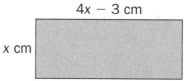
    x cm

    Perimeter = ... cm

    Perimeter = ... cm

4 If $n = 5$ and $m = 3$, calculate the values of these.

    a $n^2 = $ ....

    b $m^2 = $ ....

    c $3m^2 = $ ....

    d $2n^2 = $ ....

5 Matt the plumber uses this formula for his charges: $c = 25h + 20$
c is the total charge and h is the number of hours worked.

    How much is Matt's total charge for 5 hours work?   Answer: £ ....

N2a Mental addition and subtraction

1 Write the answers to these calculations. You can use this numberline to approximate.
The numberline shows the answer for **a**.

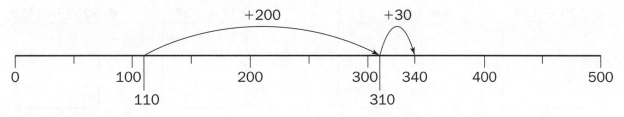

a 110 + 230 = ...   **b** 120 + 70 = ...   **c** 360 + 90 = ...   **d** 40 + 180 = ...

e 500 − 230 = ...   **f** 330 + 170 = ...   **g** 410 − 350 = ...   **h** 340 − 280 = ...

2 June has run 730 m of a 1000 m race.

0   730   1000

How much more has she to run?   Answer: .... m

3 This is a magic square. All of its rows, columns and diagonals must add up to the same number.

a What is that total?   Answer: ....

b Using your total, complete the square.

9		3	16
4		10	
	1		11
7	12		

4 Calculate the perimeters of these shapes. Try to do the calculations in your head.

a

23 m

17 m   17 m

23 m

Perimeter = ...m

b

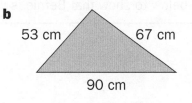

53 cm   67 cm

90 cm

Perimeter = ...cm

c

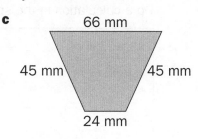

66 mm

45 mm   45 mm

24 mm

Perimeter = ...mm

1 Work out the answers to these without using a calculator.
You can use the spaces below for your working out.

a 129 + 459

b 568 + 292

c 817 + 254

d 2257 + 3419

2 Work out the answers to these subtractions without a calculator.
You can use the spaces below for your working out.

a 329 − 59

b 778 − 396

c 7657 − 1854

d 5090 − 3419

3 Challenge

BELL COMPUTERS 12.6 kg

Corn Flakes 4.9 kg

Tipps Tiles 15.4 kg

Copper pipes 8.3 kg

a Without using a calculator, work out the total weight of the four parcels.

Answer: .... kg

b How much heavier is the Bell Computer parcel than the Copper Pipe parcel?

c Bernie says that the Tiles parcel is 3·8 kg heavier than the Computer parcel.
Do a calculation in the space below to show that Bernie is wrong.

1 How good is your memory?
   Complete this multiplication grid.

×	2	4	5	7	8	9
3				21		
6		24				
7						
9					72	

2 Partition these numbers into 100's, 10's and 1's. The first one is done for you.

   a 167 = 100 + 60 + 7   **b** 325 = ... + ... + ...   **c** 54 = ... + ...

   d 89 = ... + ...   **e** 506 = ... + ... + ...   **f** 78 = ... + ...

3 Partition these numbers to multiply them.

   a 56×4

   b 67×6

   c 89×4

   d 423×7

4 Divide these numbers as quickly as you can.

   a $35 \div 5 =$ ....   **b** $36 \div 6 =$ ....   **c** $24 \div 8 =$ ....   **d** $56 \div 8 =$ ....

   e $45 \div 9 =$ ....   **f** $81 \div 9 =$ ....   **g** $60 \div 10 =$ ....   **h** $63 \div 9 =$ ....

5 Work out these divisions using your own method.

   a $92 \div 4 =$ ....   **b** $96 \div 6 =$ ....   **c** $72 \div 4 =$ ....   **d** $120 \div 6 =$ ....

   e $125 \div 5 =$ ....   **f** $135 \div 5 =$ ....   **g** $246 \div 6$ ....   **h** $344 \div 8 =$ ....

1 Multiply each of these numbers by 26. Use any method that you like.
Show your calculations by the answer boxes.
The first one is done for you by the grid method.

×	20	6
8	160	48

160 + 48 = 208

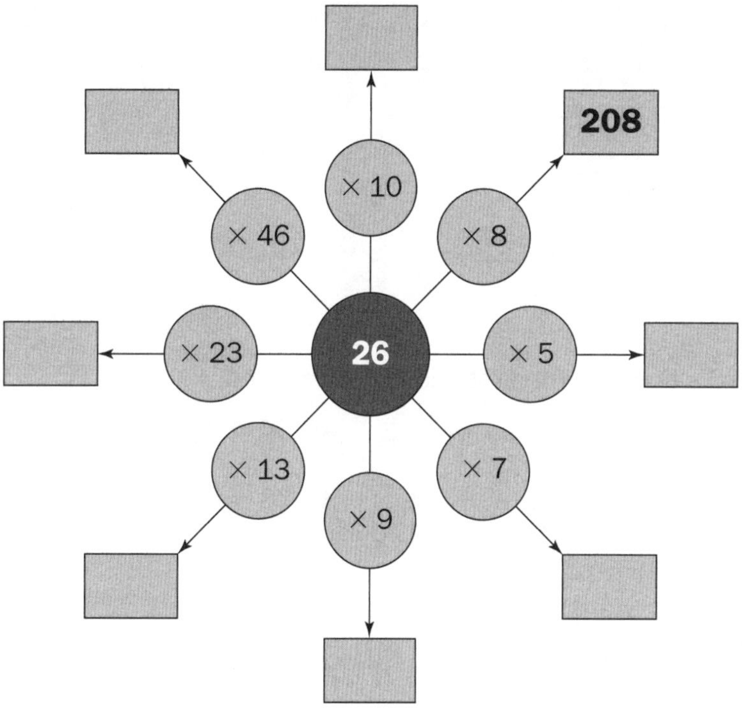

208

× 10

× 46

× 8

× 23

26

× 5

× 13

× 7

× 9

2 Jamal makes 8 sandwiches in 24 minutes.
  a How long does it take him to make one sandwich?

Answer: .... minutes

  b How many sandwiches could he make in 60 minutes?

Answer: .... sandwiches

3 Do these divisions without a calculator. Show your working in the boxes below.

a 207 ÷ 9	**b** 441 ÷ 7	**c** 416 ÷ 8	**d** 171 ÷ 9

1 How long is each line?

a

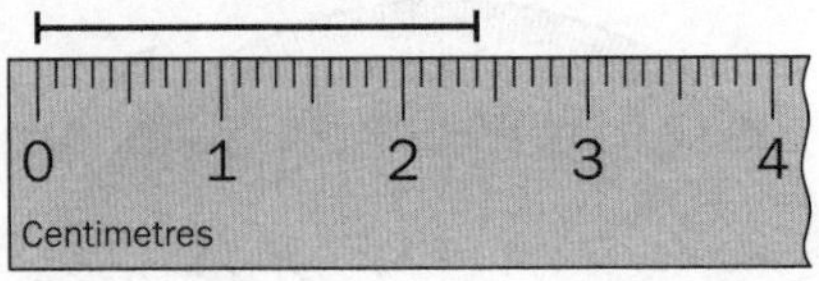

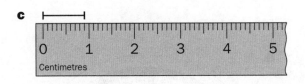

.... cm

b

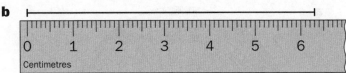

.... cm

c

Centimetres

.... cm

d

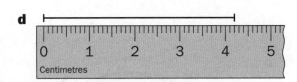

.... cm

e

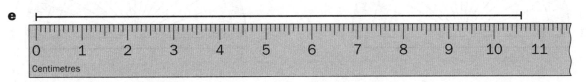

.... cm

2 Line **R** ├──────────────┤

Line **S** ├────────────────────┤

Line **T** ├──────┤

Line **U** ├──────────────┤

Line **V** ├──────────────────────────┤

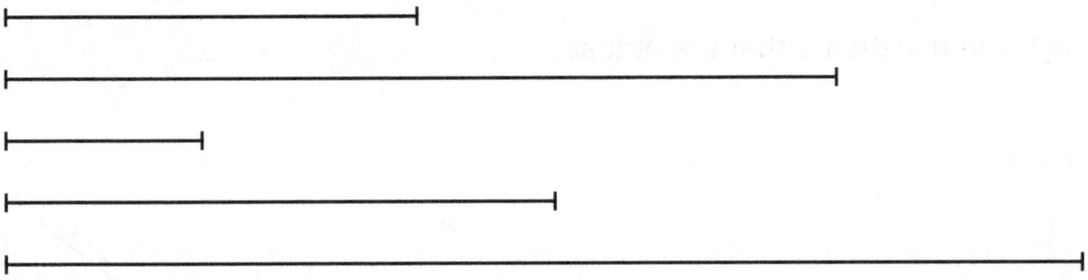

a How long is line S plus line U? ....

b How long is line V plus line R? ....

c How long is line T plus line R? ....

d How long is line V plus line S? ....

e How long is line T plus line U, plus line V? ....

3 Carefully complete these lines.

Line **a** is 5.5 cm ▬──

Line **b** is 9.3 cm ▬─

Line **c** is 4.9 cm ▬─

Line **d** is 6.7 cm ▬─

Line **e** is 11.6 cm ▬──

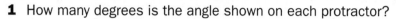

1 How many degrees is the angle shown on each protractor?

a

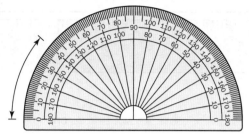

.... °

b

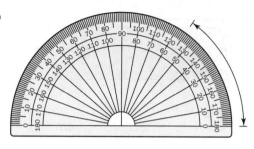

.... °

c

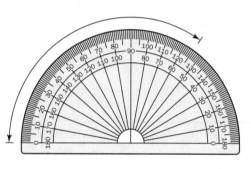

.... °

d

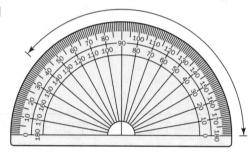

.... °

2 a List those angles in question 1 that are acute. ....

  b List those angles in question 1 that are obtuse. ....

3 Measure each angle.

a

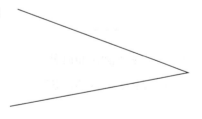

.... °

b

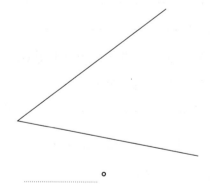

.... °

c

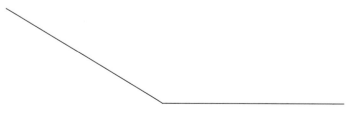

.... °

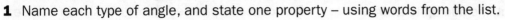

1 Name each type of angle, and state one property – using words from the list.

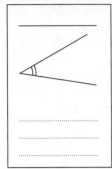 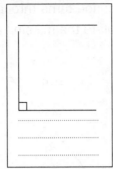 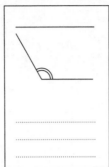 

more than 180° - right angle - less than 90° - obtuse

acute - exactly 90° - between 90° and 180° - reflex

2 Using a ruler, decide which line is parallel to line AB.

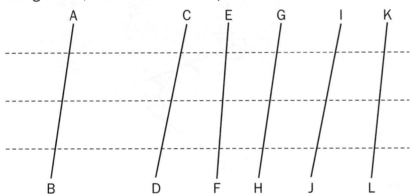

.... is parallel to AB

3 a Which line is parallel to TU? ....

  b Which line is perpendicular to TU? ....

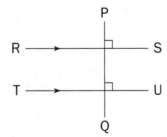

4 Draw a line parallel to AB, 2.5 cm below. Label it CD.
  Draw symbols to show the lines are parallel.

A   B

1 **Angles on a straight line add up to 180°**

Calculate the missing angle.

$a = $ ....

$b = $ ....

$c = $ ....

2 **Angles round a point add up to 360°**

Calculate the missing angle.

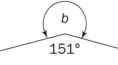

$a = $ ....

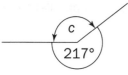

$b = $ ....

$c = $ ....

3 **Vertically opposite angles are equal**

Calculate the missing angle.

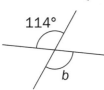

$a = $ ....

$b = $ ....

$c = $ ....

4 A canoe is paddled through a slalom course. The canoe turns through many angles.

Calculate the missing angles.

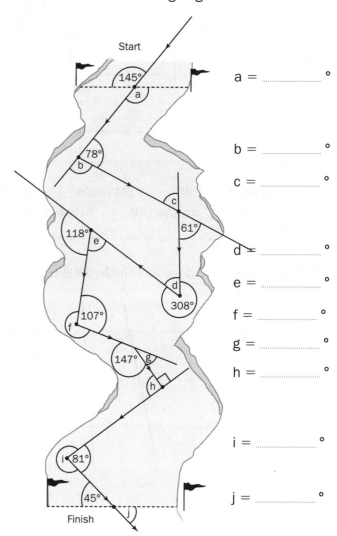

$a = $ .... °

$b = $ .... °

$c = $ .... °

$d = $ .... °

$e = $ .... °

$f = $ .... °

$g = $ .... °

$h = $ .... °

$i = $ .... °

$j = $ .... °

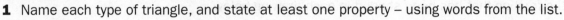

G2e Angles in a triangle

1 Name each type of triangle, and state at least one property – using words from the list.

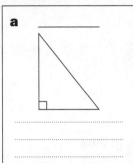

a _____

....

....

....

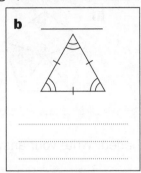

b _____

....

....

....

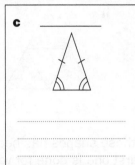

c _____

....

....

....

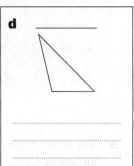

d _____

....

....

....

> scalene - 3 equal angles - no equal angles - right angle - no equal sides - isosceles
> one 90° angle - 2 equal sides - 2 equal angles - 3 equal sides - equilateral

2 Write the letter of the angle that completes each triangle.

V 90° **W** 68° **X** 125° **Y** 31° **Z** 139°

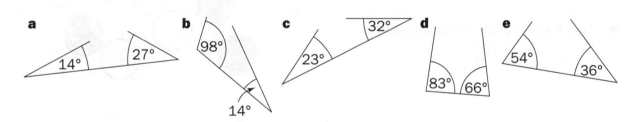

a 14° 27° **b** 98° 14° **c** 23° 32° **d** 83° 66° **e** 54° 36°

3 Use what you know about angle facts
to find angles *a*, *b* and *c*.

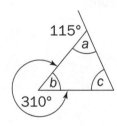

115°
a
b *c*
310°

a = ... °   b = ... °   c = ... °

ANGLES IN A TRIANGLE   23

1 a Find the fraction that has been shaded in each drawing below.

i   **ii**   **iii**

....

b Say what fraction of these shapes has been shaded. Write your answers in their
simplest form. The first one is done for you.

i 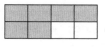   **ii**   **iii**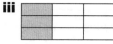

$\dfrac{6}{8} = \dfrac{3}{4}$ ....

c Shade $\dfrac{4}{5}$ of this shape.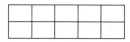

2 a What fraction of these beads are blue?

....

b What fraction of the beads are white?

....

3 Bernie has 12 birthday cards.
7 cards are from friends and the rest are from relatives.
What fraction of the cards are from:

a friends   ....

b relatives?   ....

4 In a sample of 100 light bulbs, 13 bulbs are broken.

a What fraction are broken?   **b** What fraction are not broken?

....

N3b Equivalent fractions

The shaded fraction of this square can be written in two ways: $\frac{2}{4}$ or $\frac{1}{2}$

1 Part of each rectangle has been shaded.
In the spaces write the equivalent fractions shaded. The first one is done for you.

a
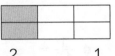

$$\frac{2}{6} = \frac{1}{3}$$

b

.... = ...

c

.... = ...

d

.... = ...

2 Write the equivalent fractions to these. The first one is done for you.

a $\frac{2}{3} = \frac{12}{18}$ (×6)

b $\frac{3}{4} = \frac{}{12}$

c $\frac{2}{5} = \frac{}{20}$

d $\frac{3}{5} = \frac{}{30}$

e $\frac{8}{10} = \frac{4}{}$

f $\frac{3}{18} = \frac{1}{}$

g $\frac{10}{20} = \frac{}{2}$

h $\frac{10}{15} = \frac{}{3}$

3 Write these improper fractions as **mixed numbers**. The first one is done for you.

a $\frac{10}{9} = 1\frac{1}{9}$

b $\frac{7}{5} = $ ....

c $\frac{11}{6} = $ ....

d $\frac{13}{9} = $ ....

e $\frac{9}{3} = $ ....

f $\frac{15}{5} = $ ....

4 When you add these fractions your answers will be **improper fractions**.
Give your final answer as mixed numbers.

a $\frac{7}{9} + \frac{4}{9} = \frac{}{9} = $ ....

b $\frac{5}{8} + \frac{5}{8} = \frac{}{8} = $ ....

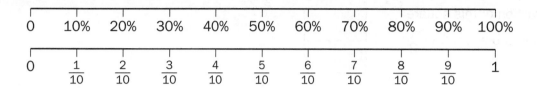

N3c Fractions and percentages

```
0    10%   20%   30%   40%   50%   60%   70%   80%   90%   100%
```

```
0    1     2     3     4     5     6     7     8     9     1
     10    10    10    10    10    10    10    10    10
```

1 Use the number lines above to write these fractions as percentages.
Use the spaces provided.

a $\frac{3}{10}$ = ... % **b** $\frac{6}{10}$ = ... % **c** $\frac{8}{10}$ = ... % **d** $\frac{1}{10}$ = ...%

2 Write these percentages as fractions. Complete the fractions.

a 10% = $\frac{}{10}$ **b** 70% = $\frac{}{10}$ **c** 20% = $\frac{}{10}$ **d** 50% = $\frac{}{10}$ **e** 90% = $\frac{}{10}$

3 Convert these percentages into hundredth fractions.

a 15% = $\frac{}{100}$ **b** 35% = $\frac{}{100}$ **c** 75% = $\frac{}{100}$ **d** 65% = $\frac{}{100}$

e 19% = $\frac{}{100}$ **f** 27% = $\frac{}{100}$ **g** 55% = $\frac{}{100}$ **h** 76% = $\frac{}{100}$

4 Change these fractions into percentages. The first one is done for you.

a $\frac{23}{100}$ = 23% **b** $\frac{75}{100}$ = ... % **c** $\frac{83}{100}$ = ... % **d** $\frac{40}{100}$ = ...%

5 75% of this rectangle has been shaded. What **fraction** is still white?

....

N3d   Fractions, decimals and percentages

1 Convert these percentages into decimal numbers.
The first two are done for you.

a 20% = **0·2**

b 53% = **0·53**

c 90% = ...

d 40% = ...

e 60% = ...

f 100% = ...

2 53% means $\frac{53}{100}$. Write these percentages as fractions.

a 61% = ...

b 33% = ...

c 79% = ...

d 99% = ...

e 47% = ...

f 23% = ...

3 Write these as fractions in their **simplest form**.

a 50% = ...

b 60% = ...

c 80% = ...

d 25% = ...

e 75% = ...

f 65% = ...

4 $\frac{53}{100}$ is written as 0·53 as a decimal. Write these fractions as decimals.

a $\frac{45}{100}$ = 0· ....

b $\frac{4}{10}$ = 0· ....

c $\frac{77}{100}$ = ...

Now complete these equivalents.

d $\frac{35}{100}$ = 0· .... = ... %

e $\frac{56}{100}$ = 0· .... = ... %

5 Circle the fractions, decimal and percentage which are equivalent to $\frac{1}{2}$.

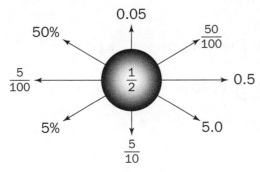

1 Draw arrows to link the equivalent operations.

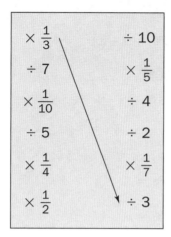

2 Work these out **without** a calculator.

a $8 \times \frac{1}{2} =$ ....

b $12 \times \frac{1}{4} =$ ....

c $15 \times \frac{1}{3} =$ ....

d $9 \times \frac{1}{3} =$ ....

e $25 \times \frac{1}{5} =$ ....

f $30 \times \frac{1}{10} =$ ....

3 If the line is 20 m long, how far has the snail travelled when it reaches

Position A .... m   Position B .... m   Position C .... m

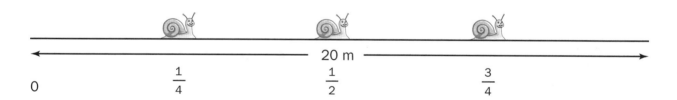

4 Calculate these fractions of amounts.

a $\frac{2}{3}$ of £30 = £ ....

b $\frac{2}{5}$ of 45 kg = ... kg

c $\frac{3}{4}$ of 120 m = ... m

d $\frac{9}{10}$ of 70 m = ... m

N3f Percentage of a quantity

When you find 10% of an amount, you can divide the amount by 10.

1 Calculate these in your head. Write your answers into the empty circles.

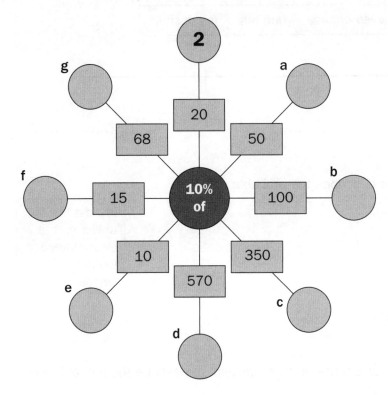

2 Complete these statements. The first one is done for you.

a 30% of an amount is **3 × 10%**

b 20% of an amount ....

c 70% of an amount is ....

d 90% of an amount is ....

e 50% of an amount is ....

f 5% of an amount is ....

You can use a calculator to work out percentages of numbers.
18% of 60 is keyed in like this:

3 Fill in these 'buttons' to show how you would key in this calculation.

27% of 95   ☐☐☐☐☐☐☐☐☐☐☐

4 Use a calculator to work out these percentages.

a 25% of 15kg = ... kg

b 45% of 88 m² = ... m²

c 21% of €68 = € ....

d 60% of £90 = £ ....

e 33% of £99 = £ ....

f 80% of 128*l* = ... *l*

1 Write the words describing probable outcomes onto the probability scale below.

> *likely - certain - even chance - unlikely - impossible*

0   1

....

....

2 Match the definition with the word that describes the probable outcome.

a The event will definitely happen _____

b Poor chance _____

c Good chance _____

d The event will never happen _____

e There is a 50/50 chance it will happen _____

> impossible
> unlikely
> even chance
> likely
> certain

3 Use the words 'impossible, unlikely, even chance, likely or certain' to describe the probability of these events.

a You have a name _____

b By flapping your arms you can fly around the room _____

c The next person you talk to will be female _____

d You roll a dice and get a '6' _____

e You will eat something in the next 12 hours _____

f You will find a £20 note on the pavement as you walk home _____

g You were born _____

h You will have a job in the future _____

4 Suggest an outcome that has an **impossible** probability.

_____

5 Suggest an outcome that has a **certain** probability.

_____

1 Use the probability scale to answer these questions.

| 0 | 0.1 | 0.2 | 0.3 | 0.4 | 0.5 | 0.6 | 0.7 | 0.8 | 0.9 | 1 |

What is the probability of picking a white ball at random from each bag?
There are 10 balls in each bag.

a

b
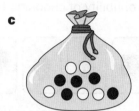

c

d

e
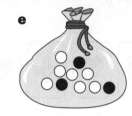

f
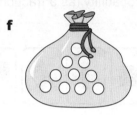

2 Use the probability scale to answer these questions.

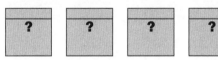

a The Golden Key is hidden in one of these boxes.

| ? | ? | ? | ? | ? |

As a fraction, what is the probability of choosing the 'winning box'? ....

b A die has 6 faces.

As a fraction, what is the probability of 'throwing' an odd number? ....

c There are 100 tickets sold for a raffle. There are 4 prizes to be won.

i I buy one ticket. What is my probability of winning a prize? ....

ii I buy four tickets. What is my probability of winning a prize? ....

1

   a How many possible outcomes are there? ....

   b What is the probability of choosing the triangle card (▲), at random? ....

2

   a How many possible outcomes are there? ....

   b What is the probability (as a fraction) of choosing the arrow card (↓), at random? ....

3

   a How many possible outcomes are there? ....

   b What is the probability (as a fraction) of choosing a cross card (✚), at random? ....

   c What is the probability (as a fraction) of choosing a heart card (♥), at random? ....

4 Answer the questions about this spinner.

   a How many possible outcomes are there? ....

   b How many successful outcomes are there? ....

   c Write the probability of a successful outcome as a fraction. ....

Probability of an event happening = $\dfrac{\text{number of favourable outcomes}}{\text{total number of all possible outcomes}}$

1 A favourable outcome is when the arrow points to 'WIN' on the spinner.

a

Number of favourable outcomes? ....
Number of possible outcomes? ....
Probability of favourable outcome? ....

b

Number of favourable outcomes? ....
Number of possible outcomes? ....
Probability of favourable outcome? ....

c

Number of favourable outcomes? ....
Number of possible outcomes? ....
Probability of favourable outcome? ....

d

Number of favourable outcomes? ....
Number of possible outcomes? ....
Probability of favourable outcome? ....

2 Calculate the probability of these outcomes when the arrow is spun.

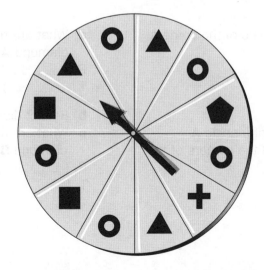

a P (▲) = ...   **b** P (■) = ...   **c** P (○ + ✚) = ...

1 Write down the coordinates of these points.

A (............ , ...)

B (............ , ...)

C (............ , ...)

D (............ , ...)

E (............ , ...)

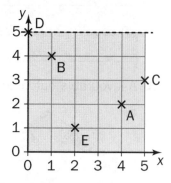

2 Add these coordinates onto the grid in question 1. Use a cross to give the exact location.

G (0 , 1)   H (4 , 0)

J (5 , 4)   K (3 , 4)

3

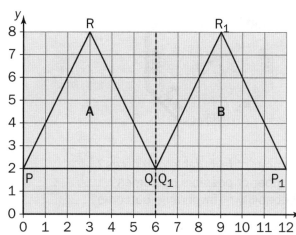

a List the three coordinates of the corners of triangle **A**.

P (............ , ...)
Q (............ , ...)
R (............ , ...)

Triangle **B** is a reflection of triangle **A**.

b List the coordinates of the corners of the reflection.

P$_1$ (............ , ...)
Q$_1$ (............ , ...)
R$_1$ (............ , ...)

4

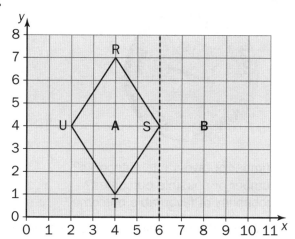

a What are the coordinates of the corners of diamond **A**?

R (............ , ...) S (............ , ...)
T (............ , ...) U (............ , ...)

b Reflect diamond **A** in the dotted line.

c What are the coordinates of the corners of diamond **B**?

R$_1$ (............ , ...) S$_1$ (............ , ...)
T$_1$ (............ , ...) U$_1$ (............ , ...)

1 Convert the coordinates below into
   letters.
   The letters make words and the words
   make a sentence.

   $(-5, 4)$ $(-6, 0)$ $(6, 6)$ T H E

   $(-2, 5)$ $(4, -2)$ $(5, 3)$ ....

   $(-2, 5)$ $(4, 0)$ $(2, 0)$ $(1, -4)$ $(-5, 0)$

   ....

   $(1, -4)$ $(2, 0)$ $(-5, 4)$

   ....

   $(-2, 5)$ $(-3, -4)$

   ....

   $(-5, 4)$ $(-6, 0)$ $(6, 6)$

   ....

   $(-6, -2)$ $(4, -2)$ $(-4, -3)$ $(6, 6)$

   ....

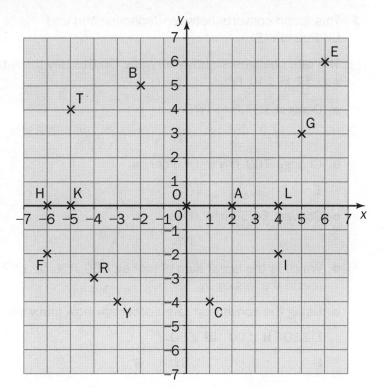

2 Plot these coordinates onto this grid.
   Plot the coordinates using a clear cross.
   Label the coordinates with the letters next
   to the brackets.

A $(0, 0)$	**B** $(4, 6)$	**C** $(-4, 5)$
D $(-6, -2)$	**E** $(-4, 1)$	**F** $(-2, 0)$
G $(0, -5)$	**H** $(3, 3)$	**J** $(4, -2)$
K $(6, 0)$	**L** $(-4, -6)$	**M** $(-3, 6)$

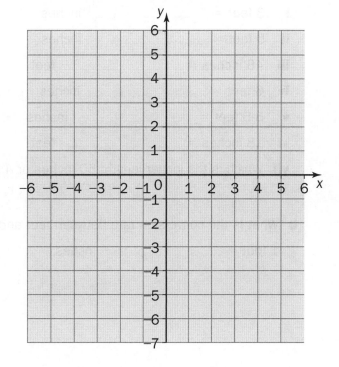

1 This graph converts between Japanese Yen and UK Pounds (£).

The rate changes slightly every day. On this day the rate was £1 ≡ 140 JYN.

a Convert £3.00 to JYN.

_____ JYN

b Change 700 JYN to UK Pounds.

£ _____

c Convert £4·50 into JYN.

_____ JYN

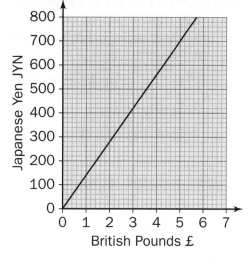

d Which is the larger sum of money, 860 JYN or £6? (circle the larger)

e Using the conversion rate above, say how many Yen you would receive if you converted

i £10 **ii** £20 **iii** £50

i _____ JYN **ii** _____ JYN **iii** _____ JYN

2 This graph converts between feet and inches.

a Use the graph to convert these:

i 3 feet = _____ inches

ii 5 feet = _____ inches

iii 48 inches = _____ feet

iv 6 feet = _____ inches

v 5·5 feet = _____ inches

vi 18 inches = _____ feet

vii Which is the longer length: 50 inches or 4 feet?

_____

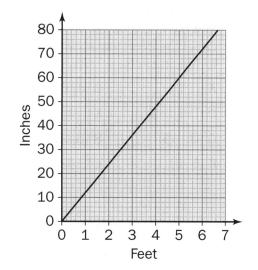

b What is the conversion rate between feet and inches?

1 foot = _____ inches

A2d More conversion graphs

1 This graph converts between temperatures in Celsius and Fahrenheit.

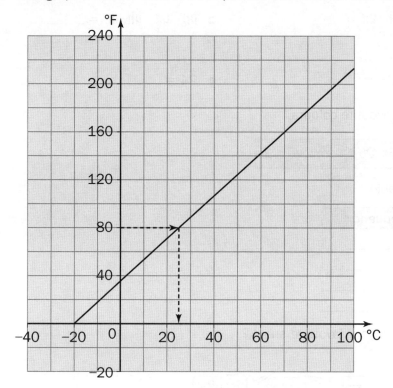

Use the graph to estimate these conversions. The first one has been done for you.

a 80°F ≈ 25°C   **b** 140° ≈ _____ °C   **c** 160°F ≈ _____ °C

d 200°F ≈ _____ °C   **e** 60°F ≈ _____ °C   **f** 100°F ≈ _____ °C

2 Estimate these temperature conversions.

a 20°C ≈ _____ °F   **b** 100°C ≈ _____ °F   **c** 30°C ≈ _____ °F

d 90°C ≈ _____ °F   **e** 10°C ≈ _____ °F   **f** −10°C ≈ _____ °F

3 Here is a list of temperatures which have been mixed up.
Rewrite them in order from the coolest to the warmest.

190°F,   40°C,   60°F,   160°F,   80°C,   −10°C,   60°C,   10°F

Coolest   Warmest

1 What number does each tally represent?

   a Ⅲ|Ⅲ ||| = ...   **b** Ⅲ|Ⅲ Ⅲ|Ⅲ = ...   **c** Ⅲ|Ⅲ Ⅲ|Ⅲ Ⅲ|Ⅲ ||| = ...

2 Show these numbers as a tally.

   a 13 = ...   **b** 19 = ...   **c** 24 = ...

3 These results are from a survey of favourite colours.

Blue = 7	Green = 5	Red = 11	Yellow = 3

Enter this data into the frequency table.

Colour	Tally	Frequency
Blue		
Green		
Red		
Yellow		

4 A group of people are asked, 'What is your favourite snack?'
Here are the replies:

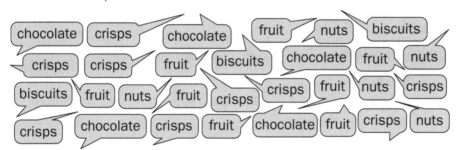

   a Organise this data into the frequency table below.

Snack	Tally	Frequency
Biscuits		
Chocolate		
Crisps		
Fruit		
Nuts		

   b How many people were surveyed? ....

   c Which is the most popular snack? ....

   d Which snack got 3 votes? ....

1 Students do a study on hair colour. They stand at the local rail station and record the hair colour of people as they pass by. Here is the data recorded.

brown	black	brown	white	blonde	blonde	brown	red	brown
black	brown	white	blonde	brown	brown	white	black	red
white	black	brown	brown	blonde	white	blonde	brown	black

a Complete the frequency table to organise this data.

Hair colour	Tally	Frequency

b Is this data collected by observation or controlled experiment?

_____

2 'Do flies prefer jam, honey or marmalade?', asked Laura.

Three plates are laid out – one with jam, one with honey and one with marmalade. For one hour the number of flies that visit each plate is recorded.

Here is the frequency table:

	Tally	Frequency
Jam	|||| |||| |||| |||| ||	
Honey	|||| |||| |||| ||||	
Marmalade	|||| |||| ||	

a Complete the table by giving the frequency.

b Which did the flies prefer? _____

c Is this data collected by observation or controlled experiment?

_____

1 The main weather features are recorded every day, over a period of time.
Here is the record shown on a two-way table.

	CLOUDY	CLEAR
WARM	4	13
COOL	6	7

a How many days were cool and cloudy? _____

b In total, how many cool days were there? _____

c How many days were warm and clear? _____

d In total, how many clear days were there? _____

e How many days were recorded, in total? _____

2 At an international athletics meeting the English team won the following
medals on the first day.

	GOLD	SILVER	BRONZE
MEN	3	0	7
WOMEN	2	5	11

a How many gold medals did the teams win, in total? _____

b Which team won 5 silver medals? _____

c How many bronze medals did the teams win, in total? _____

d How many medals did the women's team win? _____

e How many medals did the English teams win, in total? _____

3 Year 9 students have to decide which Science subject they are to take the following year.
Here are the results:

   Physics: 23 boys and 11 girls.
   Biology: 14 boys and 27 girls.
   Chemistry: 22 boys and 18 girls.

Use this data to complete this two-way table.

1 a Complete each symmetrical shape by drawing the reflection.

  b Name each completed shape.

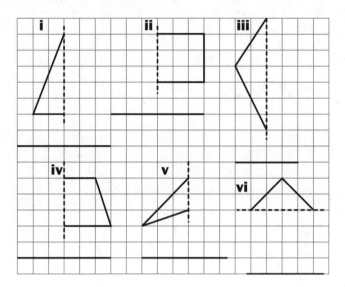

2 Draw lines of symmetry onto each shape.

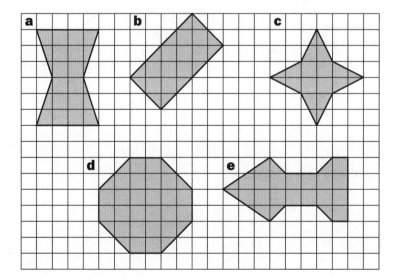

1 By joining the dots in order, draw these 3-D shapes.
Name each shape.

a

b

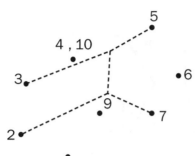

c

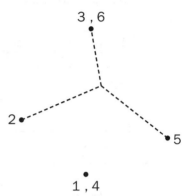

....

d

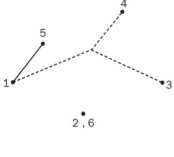

e

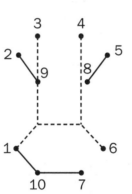

f

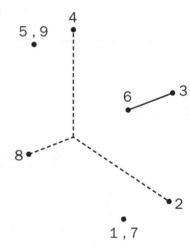

....

2 What 3-D shapes will you make if you put these faces together?

a

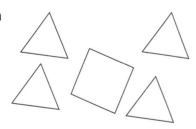

b

....

3 Name the 3-D shapes that are being described here.

a I have a square base and 4 triangular faces. ....

b I have no flat faces, no vertices or edges. ....

c I have 6 faces; all faces are square. ....

d I have 12 vertices; I have a total of 8 faces. ....

e I am composed of 2 triangular faces and 3 rectangles. ....

1 These shapes are made of 1 centimetre cubes (cm³).
What is the volume of each shape?

a

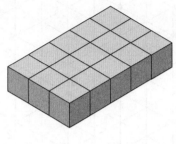

_____ cm³

b

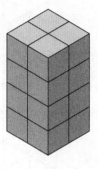

_____ cm³

c

_____ cm³

d

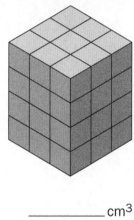

_____ cm³

e

_____ cm³

f

_____ cm³

2 Using the formula,
volume = length × width × height,
give the volume of each solid shape.

a

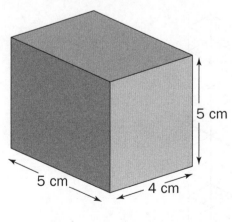

5 cm

5 cm   4 cm

_____ cm³

b

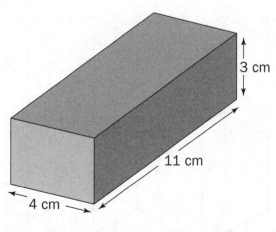

3 cm

11 cm

4 cm

_____ cm³

1 Join the dots in order to draw a 3-D cuboid shape.

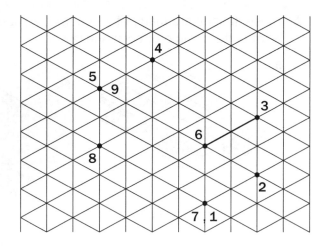

2 Copy this cuboid in 3-D.

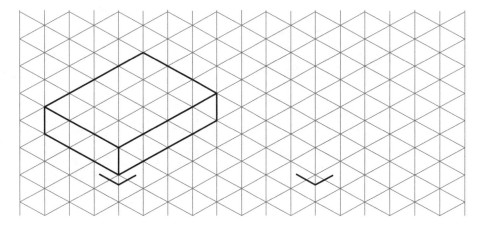

3 Copy these shapes on isometric paper.

a

b

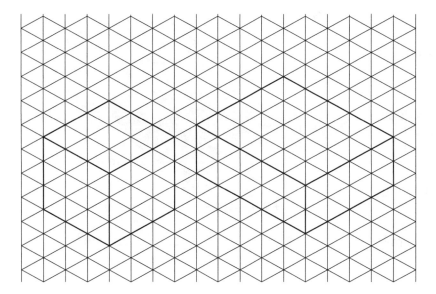

A3a Number sequences

1 a Complete the next two drawings in these tile patterns.

i   **ii**

b Continue each sequence for another three terms.

i 4, 7, 10, ..., ..., ...

ii 56 , 51, 46, ..., ..., ...

iii 7, 13, 19, ..., ..., ...

iv 9, 15, 21, ..., ..., ...

v 1 , 2 , 4 , ..., ..., ...

vi 800, 400, 200, ..., ..., ...

2 What are the term-to-term rules for these four sequences?

a 4, 9, 14, 19,   The term-to-term rule is ....

b 25, 21, 17, 13,   The term-to-term rule is ....

c 2, 4, 8, 16,   The term-to-term rule is ....

d 300, 150, 75,   The term-to-term rule is ....

3 a Generate the first four terms of a sequence by starting at 5 and adding 7.

............, ..., ..., ...

b Generate the first four terms of a sequence by starting at 21 and subtracting 3.

............, ..., ..., ...

4 Make two different sequences, each with five terms, from the numbers in the panel.
You can use numbers twice.

............, ..., ..., ...

............, ..., ..., ...

5	14	1	4
1	9	19	15
17	20	3	13

1 Write the next 4 terms of these sequences.

a 2

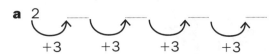

b 56

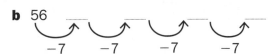

c 2

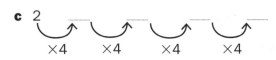

2 Write the first 4 terms of these sequences.

a Start number 5, term to term rule 'add 4' ....

b Start number 50, term to term rule 'subtract 5' ....

c Start number 1, term to term rule 'multiply by 3' ....

3 Find the missing terms. (You may use a calculator)

a 4, 8, ..., 16, 20   **b** 75, ..., 55, 45, 35,

c ...., 14, 21, 28, 35   **d** 97, 88, 79, ..., 61

e 1, 6, 36, ..., 1296   **f** 1, ..., 100, 1000, 10000

4 Write the first three terms of the sequences with the nth term given.

a $n + 2$

....
1st   2nd   3rd

b $2n - 2$

....
1st   2nd   3rd

c $3n - 1$

....
1st   2nd   3rd

d $2n + 6$

....
1st   2nd   3rd

e $4n - 3$

....
1st   2nd   3rd

f $5n + 5$

....
1st   2nd   3rd

Adding and subtracting decimals

1 Use any method that you prefer to do these calculations. Do not use a calculator.
   If it helps, you can estimate your answers first. Give accurate answers.

   a 47 + 23 = ... **b** 12 + 137 + 60 = ...

   c 87 + 29 = ... **d** 279 + 17 − 35 = ...

2 Calculate these decimal additions and subtractions. You can estimate first.

   a 1·5 + 2·9 = ... **b** 2·9 + 10·7 = ... **c** 5·6 − 2·1 = ...

   d 9·4 + 6·8 = ... **e** 22·9 + 3·3 = ... **f** 13·8 − 7·4 = ...

   g 5·8 + 1·9 = ... **h** 0·8 + 4·7 = ... **i** 15·7 − 8·9 = ...

3 The drawing show the lengths of some steel girders.

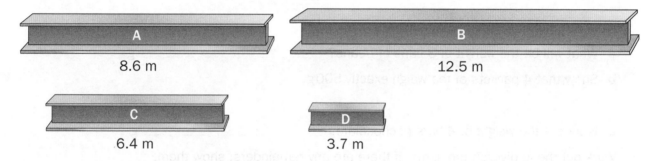

   8.6 m   12.5 m

   6.4 m   3.7 m

   Work out these lengths. Do not use a calculator.

   a girder A + girder B = ... m

   b girder D + girder C = ... m

   c How much longer is girder A than girder D? ....

   d How much longer is girder C than girder D? ....

   e How much longer is girder B than girders A and D together?

   ....

   f Show that the total length of all four girders is less than 32 m.
        Show your working here.

   g How many girders the size of **D** can be cut from girder B? ....

N4b Multiplying and dividing decimals

1 Work these out without using a calculator.

    a $17 \times 12 =$ _____   **b** $15 \times 13 =$ _____   **c** $14 \times 15 =$ _____

2 Divide these without using a calculator.

    a $180 \div 10 =$ _____   **b** $110 \div 10 =$ _____   **c** $190 \div 10 =$ _____

3 Here are three food items.

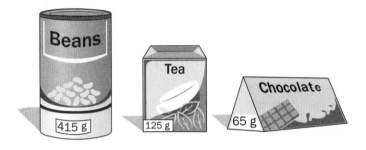

Work out these multiplication problems.

    a What will be the weight of 3 cans of beans? _____ g

    b Show that 4 packets of tea weigh exactly 500 g.

    _____

    c Work out the weight of 4 bars of chocolate. _____ g

Work out these division problems. If there are any remainders, show them.

    d How many grams will each person receive if the can of beans is shared between four people?

    _____ g

    e If the packet of tea is divided into 4 piles of equal weights, what will be the weight of each pile?

    _____ g

    f The bar of chocolate has 5 sections. What is the weight of each section?

    _____ g

4 Work out these without a calculator. There are no remainders in the divisions.

    a $4 \cdot 5 \times 10 =$ _____   **b** $14 \times 3 \cdot 2 =$ _____   **c** $7 \cdot 3 \times 5 =$ _____

    d $350 \div 5 =$ _____   **e** $640 \div 8 =$ _____   **f** $180 \div 2 \cdot 5 =$ _____

    g $27 \cdot 5 \times 6 =$ _____   **h** $81 \div 4 \cdot 5 =$ _____   **i** $280 \div 1 \cdot 4 =$ _____

1 Using a ruler, draw the reflection to complete this mask.

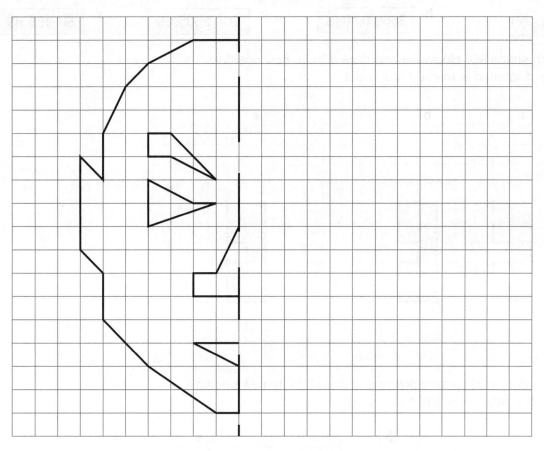

2 Draw the reflection of each shape in the mirror line.

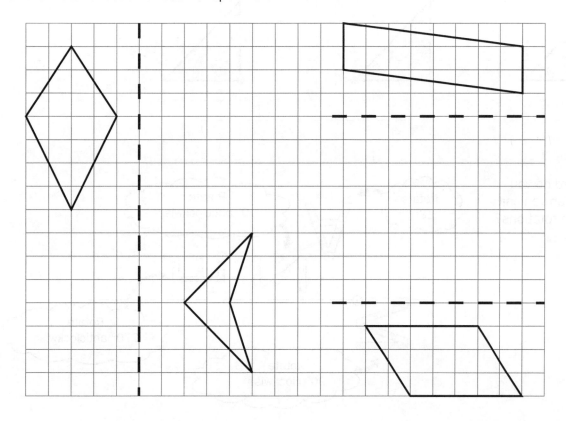

1 Tick the number plates that have rotational symmetry.

a   HOS 8 SOH   b   SMW 0 MWS   c   SOX 906 XOS   d   SH 969 HS

2 Rotate each shape 90° clockwise and draw it in its new position.
The centre of rotation is marked with a dot.

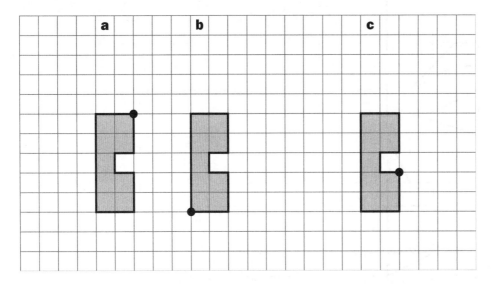

3 Rotate each shape 90° anticlockwise and draw it in its new position.
The centre of rotation is marked with a dot.

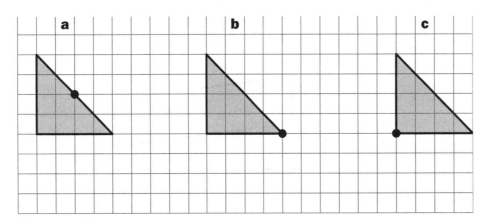

4 What word do you
make when you carry
out these rotations?

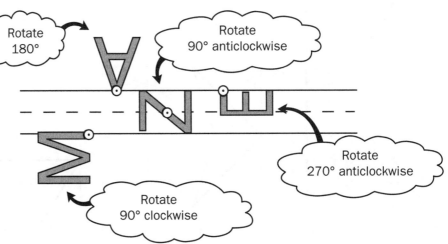

Rotate
180°

Rotate
90° anticlockwise

Rotate
270° anticlockwise

Rotate
90° clockwise

1 Translate the 'L' shape following each of these instructions.

   a 5 squares to the right, and 2 up. Draw shape and label it 'A'.

   b 6 squares to the left, and 5 down. Draw shape and label it 'B'.

   c 0 squares left or right, and 8 squares down. Draw shape and label it 'C'.

   d 8 squares to the left, and 6 squares down. Draw shape and label it 'D'.

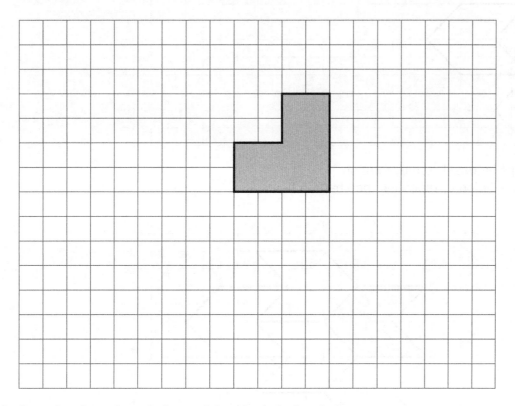

2 Describe these translations of the shaded triangle.

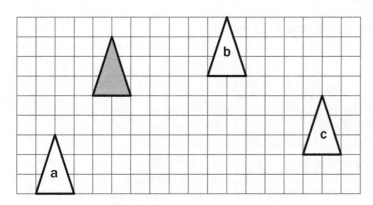

   a _____ squares to the _____, and _____ squares _____

   b _____ squares to the _____, and _____ squares _____

   c _____ squares to the _____, and _____ squares _____

1 The shaded shape is tessellated by translation ('sliding').
Continue the tessellation by repeating the shape 5 times.

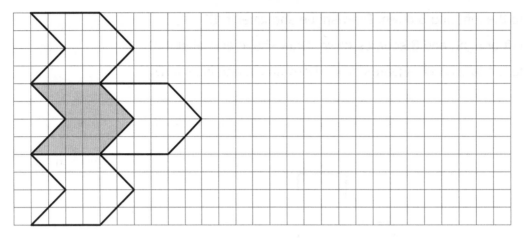

2 The shaded shape is tessellated by rotation.
Continue the tessellation by repeating the shape 5 times.

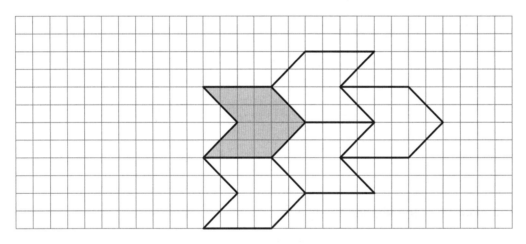

3 a Continue the tessellation by repeating this shape 5 times.

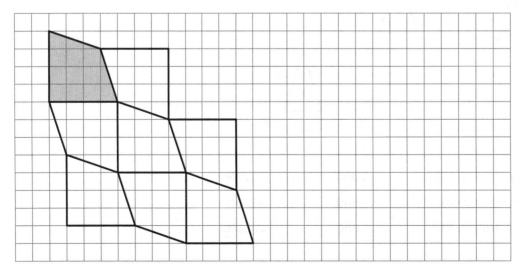

    b Is the shaded shape tessellated by translation, reflection or rotation? ....

1 To download an album from the internet the average price is about £8.99.
Calculate **the cost to the nearest £1** of these downloads.

a 10 albums: Answer: £ _____

b 7 albums: Answer: £ _____

2 Karl has a birthday party at a paintball range.
The charges are shown here:

> **Price per person: £9.99 entry fee + £7.00 for 100 paintballs**

a In the box below, calculate the cost of 100 paintballs and the entry fee for one person.

> 100 paintballs and 1 person:
>
> Total:

b Karl takes **four** friends with him. They each use 100 paintballs.
Work out the total cost.

> Total cost for **four people**:
>
> Total:

c Bernie and her sister go paintballing. They use 250 paintballs each.
Work out the total cost for Bernie and her sister.

> Bernie, her sister and their paintballs:
>
> Total:

3 A mini-cab driver is paid using this formula:

> **First mile: £3·80, extra miles are charged at £2·10 each**

Charlie takes a mini-cab from Shepherds Bush to Kingston. The journey is 10 miles.
Calculate the fare.

> Cost of the fare:
>
> Total:

1 Tony goes ten pin bowling.
The prices of shoe hire and games are shown on this sign.

Write a formula so that anyone can calculate the price for one person
to hire shoes and have any number of games.

The cost of playing ten pin bowling is:

_____ × 6 add £ _____

Prices

Shoe Hire

£2.50

Games £6.00

2

1st pattern   2nd pattern   3rd pattern   4th pattern

These patterns are made from hexagons.

a Write down the number of **solid lines** in each pattern.
Complete the number sequence below.

5, _____, _____, _____

b Write a simple formula connecting the number of **solid lines** and the pattern number.

The number of solid lines = _____ × _____

c How many **dotted lines** are there in each pattern?

Answer: _____

d Link your answers to questions **b** and **c** to write a formula to calculate the **total**
number of sticks used in any pattern number.

The **total number** of lines in any pattern =

Pattern number × _____ add _____

1 A square has four sides which are all equal in length.

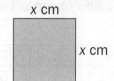

x cm

x cm

   a Write a formula for the perimeter of the square.
Use **x** as the length of one side of the square.
Simplify your answer.

   Perimeter = _____

   b Use A to represent area.
Write a formula for the area of the square.

   A = _____

2 In a military parade, soldiers march in lines with 15 soldiers per line.

   a Show how you would work out how many soldiers there would be in ten lines.

   Show your working here: Total = _____ × _____

   b How many soldiers would there be altogether in **n** lines?

   Try to simplify your answer: Total number of soldiers = _____

3 The number of chains in a fence is one less than
the number of posts used.

p stands for the number of posts used in a fence
c stands for the number of chains used

Write a formula to connect **p** and **c**. You can start
either:

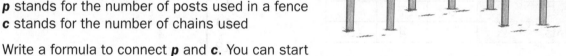

      p = _____ or

      c = _____

4 Dinesh repairs electrical goods. His hourly rate is £15 per hour and he adds a call-out charge of
£25 per customer.

   a How much will Dinesh charge for a repair taking 3 hours?

   Show your working and answer here:

   Answer: £ _____

   b Write a formula to show the total cost of a call out for any number of hours.
Use **n** for the number of hours and **C** for the total charge.
Remember the call-out charge and the hourly rate.

   Start: **C** = _____ × _____ + _____

1 a Complete the table below to convert between inches and centimetres.

inches	0	1	2	4
centimetres			5	

b Plot the values from the table onto the grid (one has been done for you).

c Use a ruler to join the points accurately onto the grid.

d Use your graph line to estimate these:

  i   3 inches ≈ _____ cm

  ii 8 cm ≈ _____ inches

  iii 3 cm ≈ _____ inches

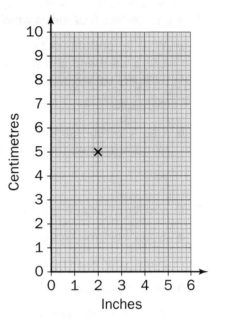

2 a Complete this table which converts pints to litres.

litres	0	7	
pints		4	8

b Plot the three pairs of coordinates onto the grid.

c Join the three points with a ruler to make a straight graph line.

d Use your graph line to convert these (you will have to estimate your answers using decimals):

  i   6 pints is about _____ litres

  ii 1 pint is about _____ litres

  iii 8 litres is about _____ pints

  iv 15 litres is about _____ pints

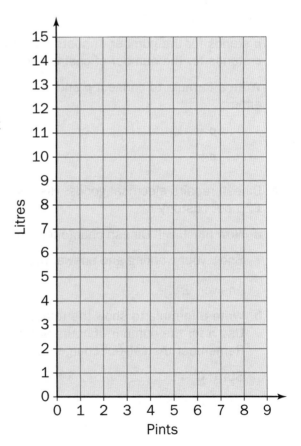

1 Rooney goes running every day.

    a Rooney starts running at .... pm.

    b How long does Rooney run before he rests?

    .... minutes

    c Rooney takes .... hours .... minutes to
return home.

    d Altogether, Rooney runs .... km

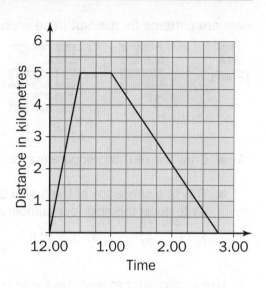

2 The graph shows a train journey.

    a The train starts off at .... am.

    b After travelling for .... minutes,

    it .... for 20 minutes.

    c The train travels a total distance of

    .... kilometres in .... hours.

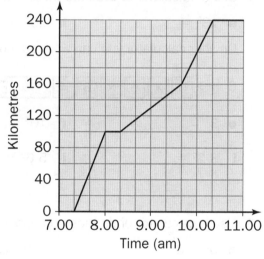

3 The four lines represent different journeys.
The arrows show the direction.

    a Which journey is the fastest?

    ....

    b Which is the 'return' journey?

    ....

    c Which journey is impossible?

    ....

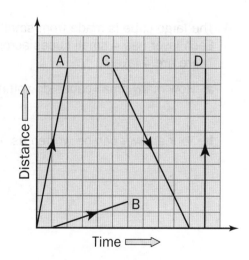

Here are patterns for the first three square numbers.

$1^2 = 1$

$2^2 = 4$

$3^2 = 9$

1 a Draw the next two square number patterns into the space above.

b This is a sequence of the first 5 square numbers.
Write down the next four numbers in the sequence.

1,   4,   9,   16,   25, ..., ..., ..., ...

2 Use a calculator to evaluate these numbers.

a $13^2 =$ ....

b $20^2 =$ ....

c $15^2 =$ ....

d $25^2 =$ ....

On your calculator you can work out cube numbers like this:

$6^3 \rightarrow$ [6] [×] [6] [×] [6] [=] [216]

e $3^3 =$ ....

f $10^3 =$ ....

g $8^3 =$ ....

h $7^3 =$ ....

i $3{\cdot}2^2 =$ ....

j $5{\cdot}6^2 =$ ....

k $3{\cdot}2^3 =$ ....

l $1{\cdot}6^3 =$ ....

3 Use a calculator or do these on paper to find the value of these expressions.

a $5^2 - 3^2 =$ ....

b $10^3 + 13^2 =$ ....

c $7^3 - 9^2 =$ ....

4 The large cube is made from smaller centimetre cubes.
Each layer has 4 small cubes across and 4 cubes deep.
There are 4 layers.

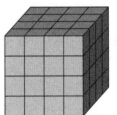

a How many small cubes do you need to make a big cube?

....

b Your answer can be written as $4^{\square}$. What number goes into the box?

....

N5b   Factors and multiples

1 Complete these factor diagrams.

a 16

1	2	4

b 24

1	2	3	4

Find all the factor pairs for these numbers and complete the factor diagrams.

c 18

d 40

2 a Find as many factors as you can for these numbers.

  i   15: ....

  ii 36: ....

  iii 60: ....

b Circle the factors which are common to 36 and 60.

3

Factors of 40   Factors of 50

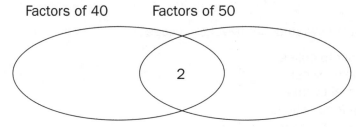

2

a i List the factors of 40 in this ring.   **ii** List the factors of 50 in this ring.

b List the common factors in the cross-over of both rings. For example, 2.

4 a List the first ten multiples of 4.

  4: 4, ..., ..., ..., ..., ..., ..., ..., ..., ...,

b List the first ten multiples of 6.

  6: 6, ..., ..., ..., ..., ..., ..., ..., ..., ...,

Circle the common multiples in each list.

1 A survey is carried out in a village. The question is:
'How many cars are there at your household?'
Here is a pictogram of the results.

Key:

🚗 = 10 houses

🚗 = 5 houses

Cars per house	Number of households
No car	🚗 🚗
1 car	🚗 🚗 🚗 🚗 🚗 🚗
2 cars	🚗 🚗 🚗
3 cars	🚗
more than 3 cars	🚗

a How many houses have no car? ....

b How many houses have more than 3 cars? ....

c There is a group of 55 houses.
How many cars do each of these household have? ....

d How many households were surveyed in total? ....

2 A survey is carried out to discover how students travel to college.

Here are the results: 30 **walk** to college
25 travel by **car**
65 travel by **bus**
40 **cycle** to college
35 travel by **train**

Display this data on the pictogram, using the key.

Key:

♀ = 10 students

♀ = 5 students

Type of travel	Number of students
Walk	
Car	
Bus	
Cycle	
Train	

a How many students were surveyed in total? ....

b How many students use public transport? ....
(public transport = buses and trains)

1 The frequency table shows the results of a survey about hair colour.
   Transfer this data onto the bar chart.

   a Label the columns (the bars)

   b Put number on the *y* axis

   c Label the *x* axis, 'Colour of hair'

   d Label the *y* axis, 'Number of people'

Hair colour	Tally	Frequency
Black	IIII II	7
Blonde	IIII	4
Brown	IIII IIII II	12
Red	III	3
White	IIII I	6

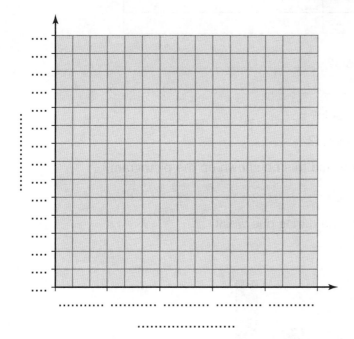

2 This is the number of portions of fish sold at Bert's Fish Bar, during one evening.

   9 haddock – 4 huss – 13 cod – 2 skate – 5 plaice

   On the grid below, draw a bar chart to show this data.

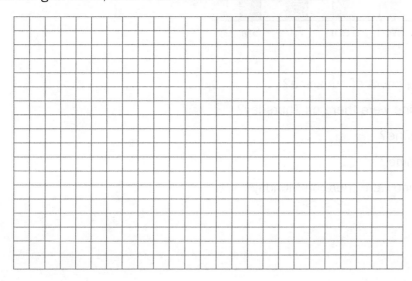

1 The pictogram shows how many sandwiches were sold in the canteen.

Sandwich	Number sold
Chicken	⬭⬭⬭⬭⬭⬭◗
Beef	⬭⬭⬭⬭
Cheese	⬭⬭⬭⬭⬭◗
Bacon	⬭⬭⬭
Sardine	⬭◗
Egg	

Key:
⬭ = 4 sandwiches

a How many beef sandwiches were sold? ....

b Which sandwich sold the most? ....

c How many cheese sandwiches were sold? ....

d How many sardine sandwiches were sold? ....

e 10 egg sandwiches were sold. How would this be shown on the pictogram?

2 The bar chart shows the hours of sunshine during one week.

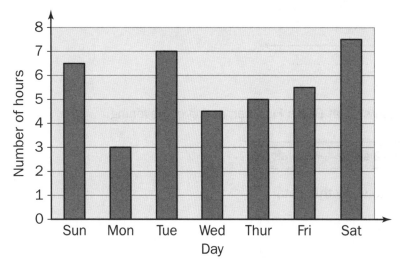

a On which day was there $5\frac{1}{2}$ hours of sunshine? ....

b How many hours of sunshine were there on Thursday? ....

c Which day had most sunshine? ....

d Which day had least sunshine? ....

e How many hours of sunshine were there on Monday? ....

1 In their 'mock' Maths exams, a group of students achieved grades between 'A' and 'E'.
The comparative bar chart shows how many students achieved each grade.

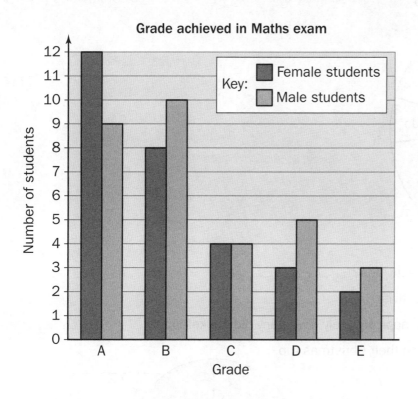

a How many boys got grade 'B' in the exam? ....

b How many girls got grade 'B' in the exam? ....

c How many students achieved grade 'C'? ....

d What grade did five of the boys attain? ....

e At which grade did girls achieve more passes than boys? ....

f How many boys took the exam? ....

g How many girls took the exam? ....

h How many students achieved grades A to C? ....

1 At Sports Expo, students spend half a day doing the sport of their choice.
The pie charts shows attendance figures at each activity.

Attendance at Sports Expo

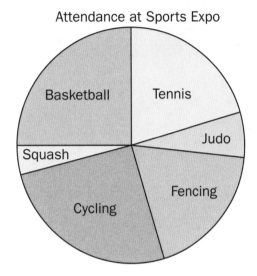

a Which were the most popular activities? ....

b Which was the least popular activity? ....

c If 100 students were involved, approximately how many did basketball? ....

2 Members of a Youth Group vote on their Christmas trip.

These are the votes:

Ice skating = 10 votes
Circus   = 8 votes
Cinema   = 27 votes
Fun Fair   = 12 votes
Swimming   = 3

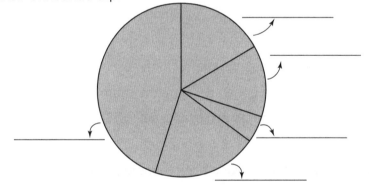

Look carefully at the pie chart and decide which section represents each activity. Label each section.

3 Fill in this pie chart to describe your day.
What part of 24 hours do you spend:

a sleeping

b working/studying

c eating

d watching TV

e time with friends

f free time?

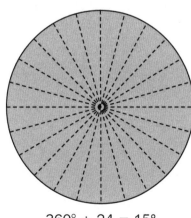

360° ÷ 24 = 15°
Each sector (1 hour) = 15°

1 The temperature in a supermarket refrigerator is recorded every hour.

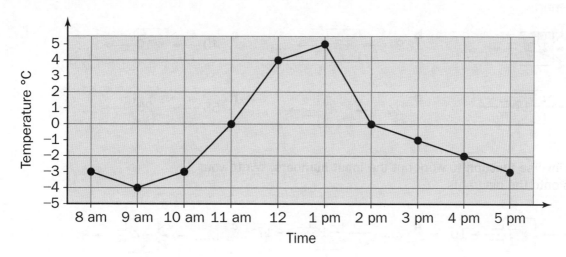

a What time is the refrigerator coldest? ....

b What is the temperature at 3 pm? ....

c The refrigerator breaks down. What time do you think this happens? ....

d The refrigerator is repaired. What time do you think this is done? ....

e How many degrees difference is there between the highest
and lowest temperatures? ....

2 The number of customers in a café is recorded every hour. Here is the data.

Time	9 am	10 am	11 am	12	1 pm	2 pm	3 pm	4 pm	5 pm	6 pm
Number of customers	12	5	3	9	17	15	2	3	7	13

Plot this data onto the time series graph.

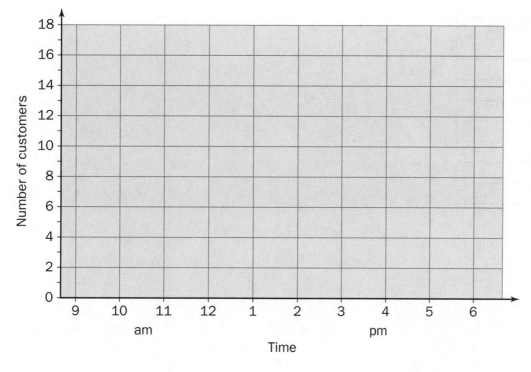

1 Write the **outputs** from these function machines onto the diagrams.

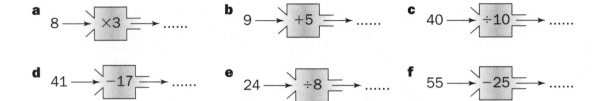

a 8 ⟶ ×3 ⟶ ......

b 9 ⟶ +5 ⟶ ......

c 40 ⟶ ÷10 ⟶ ......

d 41 ⟶ −17 ⟶ ......

e 24 ⟶ ÷8 ⟶ ......

f 55 ⟶ −25 ⟶ ......

2 Use the **inverse function** to work out the **input numbers**. Write your
answers onto the diagrams.

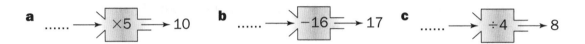

a ...... ⟶ ×5 ⟶ 10

b ...... ⟶ −16 ⟶ 17

c ...... ⟶ ÷4 ⟶ 8

3 There are two possible functions for each machine below.
Write **both** functions into the machines.

a 8 ⟶ ⟶ 40

b 50 ⟶ ⟶ 10

4 Use this function machine to complete the
input / output table below.

⟶ ÷3 ⟶

Input	Output
6	
9	
30	
24	
27	
3	
60	
72	

1 Answer these problems for the Thinker!

a

What number added to 9 makes 15?

....

b

What number do I add to 7 to make 10?

....

c

What number should I add to 24 to make 30?

....

d

If I take my number from 20, I get 11. What is my number?

....

e

When I add 74 to my number I get 100. What is my number?

....

f

When I subtract 20 from my number I get 80. What is my number?

....

2 Complete these calculations.

a 7 +......... = 10   **b** 12 −......... = 8   **c** 15 −......... = 5

d .... − 5 = 15   **e** 30 +......... = 72   **f** .... − 15 = 45

3 Use the ideas above to find the input values for these function machines.

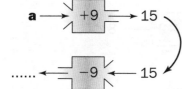

a → +9 → 15
...... ← −9 ← 15

b → −5 → 8
...... ← +5 ← 8

c → −16 → 30
...... ← +16 ← 30

4 Use inverse thinking to solve these equations (find the value of the letter).

a m + 7 = 10   **b** t − 5 = 5   **c** 12 + k = 20   **d** 15 − j = 10

m = ...   t = ...   k = ...   j = ...

e g + 15 = 21   **f** v + 25 = 40   **g** 24 − q = 16   **h** 15 + z = 30

g = ...   v = ...   q = ...   z = ...

1 Answer these multiplication and division problems for the 'Thinker'!

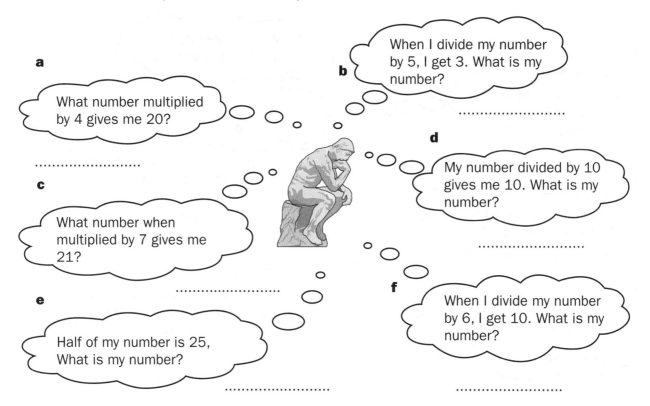

a What number multiplied by 4 gives me 20?

....

b When I divide my number by 5, I get 3. What is my number?

....

c What number when multiplied by 7 gives me 21?

....

d My number divided by 10 gives me 10. What is my number?

....

e Half of my number is 25, What is my number?

....

f When I divide my number by 6, I get 10. What is my number?

....

2 Complete these calculations.

a $7 \times$ .... $= 28$ **b** $24 \div$ .... $= 8$ **c** $15 \times$ .... $= 75$

d .... $\div 5 = 20$ **e** .... $\times 9 = 45$ **f** .... $\div 15 = 4$

3 Use the ideas above to find the input values for these function machines.

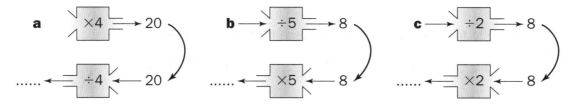

4 Use inverse thinking to solve these equations (find the value of the letter).

a $3m = 30$ **b** $10p = 60$ **c** $5h = 20$ **d** $\frac{r}{5} = 10$

   $m =$ .... $p =$ .... $h =$ .... $r =$ ....

e $6 = \frac{y}{4}$ **f** $\frac{m}{15} = 2$ **g** $30j = 60$ **h** $\frac{x}{20} = 10$

   $y =$ .... $m =$ .... $j =$ .... $x =$ ....

1 Calculate the weight of the grey shapes which will make the drawings balance.
Write your answers onto the grey shapes.

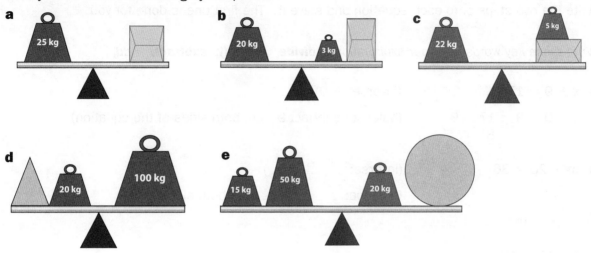

2 By balancing, work out the weight of the grey shapes in each diagram.

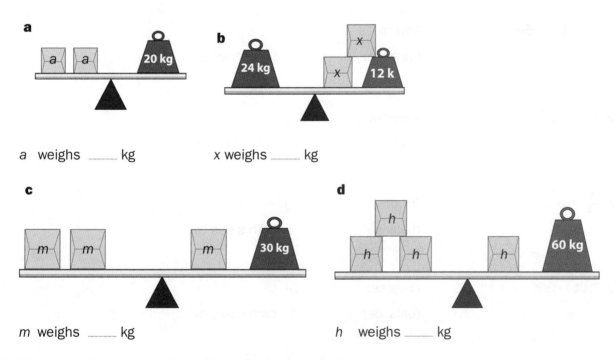

a weighs .... kg   *x* weighs .... kg

m weighs .... kg   *h* weighs .... kg

3 There are the same number of biscuits in each packet.
Use balancing to work out how many biscuits there are in a packet.

2 packets and 9 biscuits = 3 packets and 1 biscuit

....

THE BALANCE METHOD   69

1 Imagine that you are showing a friend how to solve equations using inverses and balancing.
Write the two steps onto each equation and solve it. The first one is done for you.

Write these key words into your explanations: **divide, multiply, subtract, add,**

a $x + 9 = 17$ (inverse: $- 9$)

   $x + 9 - 9 = 17 - 9$ (balance: subtract 9 from both sides of the equation)
                $\underline{x = 8}$

b $m + 20 = 36$ (inverse: ....)

                  $=$ (balance: .... from both sides)

            $m = $ ....

c $f - 17 = 13$ (inverse: ....)

                  $=$ (balance: .... to both sides)

            $f = $ ....

d $k - 14 = 56$ (inverse: ....)

                  $=$ (balance: .... to both sides)

            $k = $ ....

e $5m = 35$ (inverse: ....)

                  $=$ (balance: .... both sides by ....)

            $m = $ ....

f $\dfrac{g}{8} = 6$ (inverse: ....)

                  $=$ (balance: .... both sides by ....)

            $g = $ ....

g $10t = 360$ (inverse: ....)

                  $=$ (balance: .... both sides by ....)

            $t = $ ....

Reflections 2

1 Reflect the shape in the *y* axis.

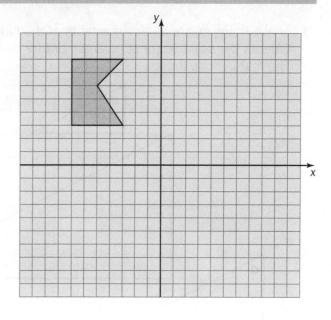

2 Reflect the shape in the dotted line.

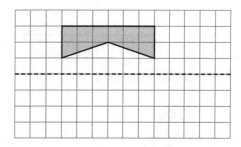

3 Reflect this shape in the three blank quadrants.

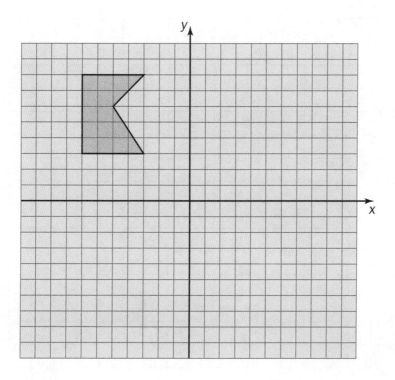

1 These triangles are all enlargements of the blue triangle.
What is the scale factor of enlargement for each triangle?
The first is done for you.

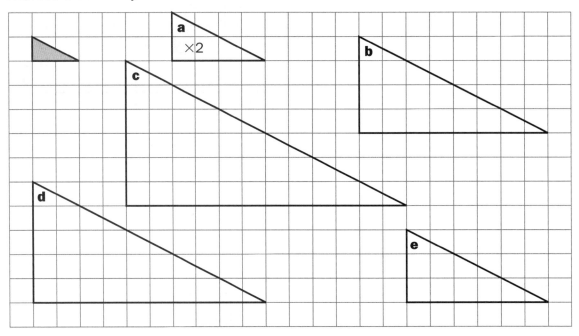

2 Re-draw this sailboat to a scale factor of 2.

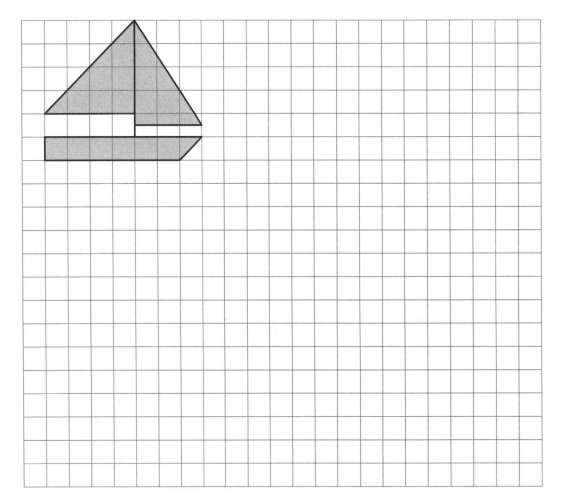

1 As fractions in their simplest terms, what proportion of each shape has been shaded?

   a 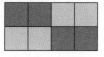   **b** 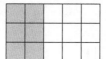   **c** 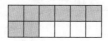   **d**

....

2 a What is the proportion of the total number of coins in each tube below?
Give your answers as fractions in the simplest terms.

   i    **ii**    **iii**

b What proportion of each jar is filled with water? Give your answers as percentages.

   i   **ii**    **iii**

3 Re-write these in order, smallest first.

   a $\frac{1}{2}$, $\frac{1}{4}$, $\frac{1}{10}$, $\frac{1}{3}$ .... , ... , ... , ...

   b 10%,   0·09, $\frac{1}{100}$,   0·25   .... , ... , ... , ...

4 In a short survey, 3 people out of a hundred said that they had no email account.
What proportion of the people surveyed said that they did not have an email
account? Give your answer as a decimal.

....

1 A builder makes a 'rough' drawing of the dimensions of a holiday chalet.

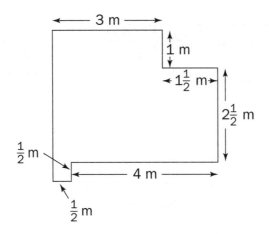

Draw an accurate plan of the chalet using the builder's measurements.

Scale:- each square = 25 cm

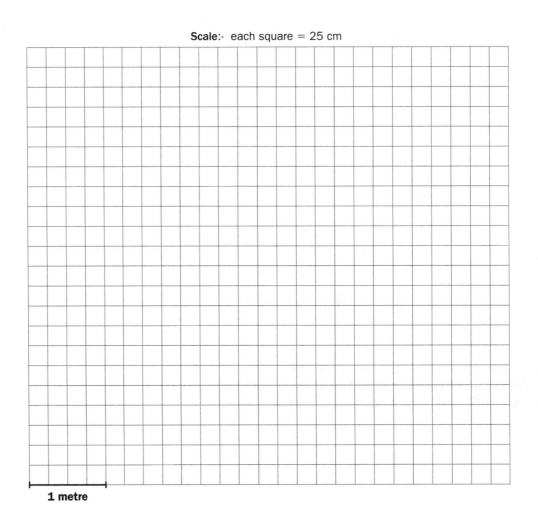

1 metre

1 Do these in your head.

a 10 × 7 = ...   **b** 15 × 10 = ...   **c** 26 × 10 = ...

d 13 × 100 = ...   **e** 280 ÷ 10 = ...   **f** 2000 ÷ 10 = ...

g 10 × 4·4 = ...   **h** 31·9 ÷ 10 = ...   **i** 26 ÷ 10 = ...

j 3·2 × 100 = ...   **k** 150 ÷ 100 = ...   **l** 605 ÷ 100 = ...

2

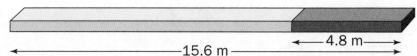

The plank is 15·6 m long. 4·8 m of the plank has been painted blue.

a In your head, work out how much of the plank is unpainted.

.... m

b Each of the 10 tiles weighs 1·9 kg. In your head, work out the total weight of all ten tiles.

.... kg

3 Use any mental method that you like to calculate these.
You can make short notes or jottings to help, but not use a calculator.

a 10 − 7·2 = ...   **b** 2·5 + 5·5 = ...   **c** 13·1 × 9 = ...

d 4·7 + 8·7 = ...   **e** 50·8 ÷ 10 = ...   **f** 12·8 × 4 = ...

g 9·2 − 4·9 = ...   **h** 354 ÷ 6 = ...   **i** 25·5 ÷ 5 = ...

j 7·2 + 19·9 = ...   **k** 72·9 ÷ 9 = ...   **l** 60·5 × 9 = ...

4 Use the fact that 2·5 x 9·6 = 24 to do these calculations.

a 25 × 9·6 = ...   **b** 250 × 9·6 = ...   **c** 2·5 × 96 = ...

d 25 × 96 = ...   **e** 0·25 × 9·6 = ...   **f** 0·25 × 96 = ...

g 24 ÷ 9·6 = ...

(there is no need to do the division, remember that 2·5 × 9·6 = 24)

h 24 ÷ 2·5 = ...   **i** 240 ÷ 2·5 = ...   **j** 240 ÷ 9·6 = ...

1 Use a written method to do these decimal additions and subtractions.
The first two are examples, but you can use your own method instead.

a 18·6 + 5·7

b 23 ·7 − 18·9

c 15 · 9 + 22 · 7 = ...

d 45 · 2 − 14 · 6 = ...

e 72 · 7 − 44 · 3 = ...

f 46 · 3 + 57 · 9 = ...

g 21 · 8 + 19 · 4 − 25 · 7 = ...

2 Complete these grids to multiply the numbers.

When multiplying with decimal numbers it is useful to estimate an answer first.

a 7·8 × 43

b 53 × 6·4

7.8 × 43

×	70	8
40	2800	
3		24

Estimate: 8 × 40 ≈ ....

Answer: ....

53 × 6.4

×	50	3
60		180
4	200	

Estimate: 50 × 7 ≈ ....

Answer: ....

3 Use the above method or a different written method to multiply these.

a 57 × 3·6 = ...

b 8·3 × 43 = ...

c 9·4 × 73 = ...

4 Use a written method to divide these numbers.
It is useful to re-write the division so that you are working with whole numbers.
Here is an example.

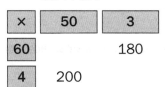

a 72 ÷ 4·5 = ...

b 84 ÷ 3·5 = ...

c 75·6 ÷ 9 = ...

d 62·3 ÷ 7 = ...

e 70·2 ÷ 7·8 = ...

1 These doughnuts need to be re-distributed evenly amongst these six boxes.

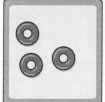 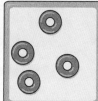  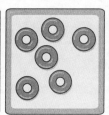 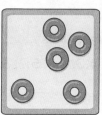 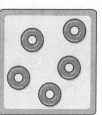

How many doughnuts will there be in each box? ....

2 These sweets are placed into five bowls.

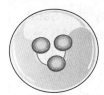 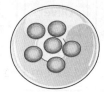 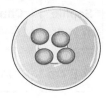 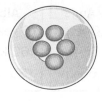 

What is the mean average number of sweets per bowl? ....

3 Ricco has played in 5 basketball matches.

He has scored: 4pts - 14 pts - 6 pts - 7 pts - 4 pts
What is the mean average score per match? ....

4 Daisy works at a travel agency. In one week, her work hours are:

Monday 7 hours – Tuesday 5 hours – Wednesday 8 hours
Thursday 8 hours – Friday 9 hours – Saturday 5 hours

As a mean average, how many hours does Mandy work each day? ....

5 Ten numbered cards are drawn at random.

| 4 | 8 | 3 | 7 | 2 | 6 | 6 | 4 | 2 | 8 |

What is the mean average of the numbers selected? ....

6 Twelve darts are thrown at this target.

What is the mean average score per dart? ....

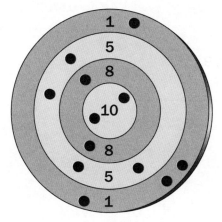

1 What is the median average for each of these numbers?

   a 8, 4, 11, 5, 5, 9, 3 _____

   The median is _____

   b 2.9, 0.9, 6.0, 4.5, 3.3, 5.7, 3.6 _____

   The median is _____

2 Nine students fill in data about their age, weight and height.
Here are the 9 data cards.

Josh	Kelly	Anne	Ali	Sophie	Charlie	Oliver	Jenny	Sarah
15 years	17 years	16 years	16 years	14 years	18 years	16 years	17 years	15 years
47 kg	51 kg	58 kg	62 kg	39 kg	71 kg	66 kg	58 kg	41 kg
168 cm	160 cm	165 cm	183 cm	148 cm	204 cm	181 cm	177 cm	164 cm

   a Write out the ages in order, smallest to biggest on the grid below.
   What is the median age?

   The median age is _____

   b Write out the weights in order, smallest to biggest on the grid below.
   What is the median weight?

   The median weight is _____

   c Write out the heights in order, smallest to biggest on the grid below.
   What is the median height?

   The median height is _____

3 A shoe shop sells 12 pairs of trainers in one day.

   The sizes of the trainers sold are: 7, 6, 6, 5, 9, 8, 7, 10, 9, 7, 8, 9
   Write out the sizes in order: _____
   What is the median average size of trainer? _____

1 What is the mode for each group of data?

   a 4, 10, 3, 2, 3, 9, 2, 3, 2, 7, 9   Mode = _____ and _____

   b 0.6, 0.6, 0.8, 0.9, 0.3, 0.8, 0.5, 0.8   Mode = _____

   c red, blue, blue, red, green, yellow, red,
       brown, red, yellow, green, red   Modal colour = _____

2 What is the range for each group of data?

   a 14, 6, 17, 22, 9, 13, 5, 20, 11, 18   Range = _____

   b 4.6, 7.2, 3.5, 8.8, 5.9, 5.3, 9.0, 6.0   Range = _____

   c 149, 68, 150, 138, 87, 67, 106   Range = _____

3 What is the mode and range of this data?

   a 2, 5, 3, 6, 5, 2, 5, 1, 1, 5   Mode = _____   Range = _____

   b 9, 11, 12, 19, 12, 13, 10, 21, 12   Mode = _____   Range = _____

   c 6, 11, 2, 6, 17, 4, 9, 2, 2, 6, 8   Mode = _____ and _____   Range = _____

4 These shoes were sold in one day at the Pinchfoot Shoe Shop.
Here are the empty shoe boxes. They show the price and shoe size on the label.

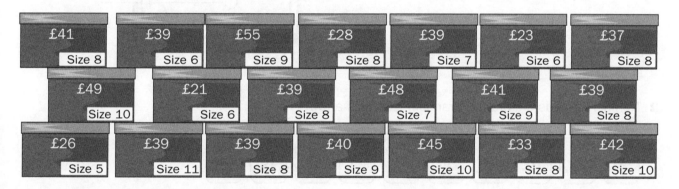

   a What is the modal average price of shoes? _____

   b What is the range of prices? _____

   c What is the modal average size of shoes? _____

   d What is the range of shoe sizes? _____

1 Use this probability scale to answer these questions.

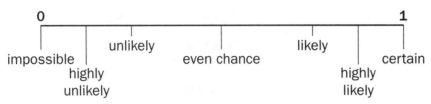

A snooker player has a choice of six balls to shoot at. Using the scale above, describe the probability of potting each ball.

Ball A = ...

Ball B = ...

Ball C = ...

Ball D = ...

Ball E = ...

Ball F = ...

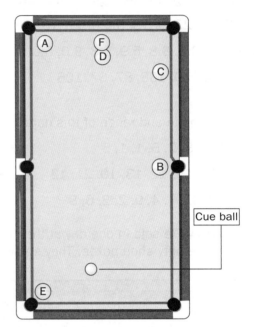

2 Numbered cards are drawn at random from this array.

a As a fraction, what is the probability of choosing the number 11 card? ....

b As a fraction, what is the probability of choosing an odd number? ....

c As a fraction, what is the probability of choosing a multiple of 5? ....

d As a fraction, what is the probability of choosing a prime number? ....

e As a fraction, what is the probability of choosing a number less than 13? ....

1 Draw the net of this cuboid.

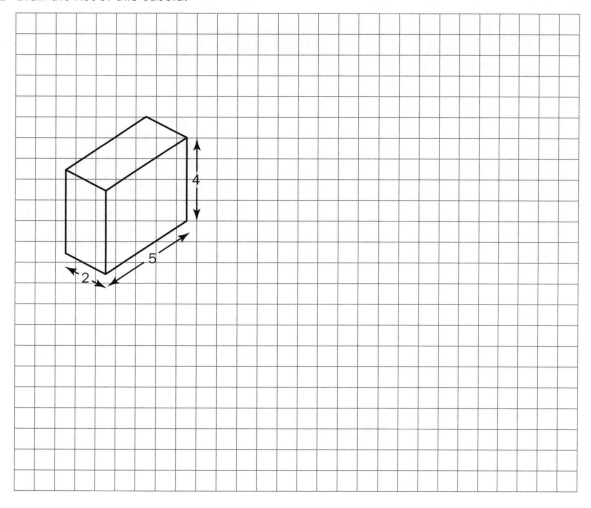

2 Use this net to make an isometric sketch of the cuboid.

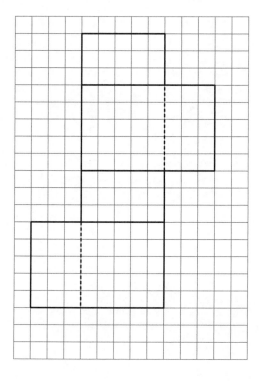